Theological Reflections at the Boundaries

Theological Reflections at the Boundaries

PAUL O. INGRAM

CASCADE *Books* · Eugene, Oregon

Cascade Books
An Imprint of Wipf and Stock Publishers
199 W. 8th Ave., Suite 3
Eugene, OR 97401

www. wipfandstock.com

ISBN 13: 978-1-61097-405-9

Cataloging-in-Publication data:

Ingram, Paul O. (1939–).

   Theological reflections at the boundaries / Paul O. Ingram.

   xii + 176 p. ; 23 cm. Including bibliographical references and index.

   ISBN 13: 978-1-61097-405-9

   1. Christianity and other religions. 2. Christianity and other religions—Buddhism. 3. Buddhism—Relations—Christianity. 4. Religious pluralism. I. Title.

BR128 I54 2012

Manufactured in the U.S.A.

Contents

10/9/2012 Yandra 39793

Preface

IT WAS ABOUT THIRTY-FIVE years ago when Christian faith began to dawn on me, when, as St. Paul said, "It pleased the Lord to reveal his Son to me." Not that I had a sudden flash of insight or heard voices or talked to Jesus as a kind of best buddy. Whenever people tell me they've talked to God or Jesus, I always feel a little creepy. Nor was my experience like being knocked off a horse, as it was for St. Paul. Nor did I catch Christian faith because of anything I studied at the Claremont School of Theology or did research on at the Claremont Graduate University. In fact, at the time, I wasn't aware that anything unusual had happened.

The occasion was a quiet conversation in 1983 I had with one of my teachers under an escalator in a New Orleans hotel lobby during a national meeting of the American Academy of Religion. My theology professor at the Claremont School of Theology, John Cobb, had just published a book titled *Christ in a Pluralistic Age*. One chapter in this book called for dialogue between Christians and Buddhists. It was a wonderfully cutting edge piece of theological reflection, but I didn't agree with some of his interpretations of Buddhism. So I wrote a critical review essay and sent it to him in advance of submitting it for publication in order to give him a chance to tell me if I had misinterpreted or misunderstood his methodology or conclusions. Our first chance to talk was in New Orleans, sitting on the floor under an escalator in the main lobby of the conference hotel.

I was surprised and gratified that he liked what I had written—and the fact that I had written it—even though he thought some of my critique had missed several points he was trying to make. Our conversation was intense and serious, which is always John's way of dealing with people he trusts. What I remember most about our conversation was my defensiveness about Christian tradition in general. Once, when I interviewed for my faculty position at Pacific Lutheran University, the Department Chair asked me if I considered myself a Christian. I took a deep breath and said, "My problem with that question is that most people who publicly identify themselves as Christian are so obnoxious about it." There was a great silence. "Especially now," I continued, "when so many people who talk about Christian faith in public seem to regard 'Christian' as synonymous with 'fundamentalism'"—a heresy the media seems hell-bent on perpetuating. Today, the fact that Islam is treated with the same ignorance offers me no comfort. So I continue to wonder if being a Christian is something we should claim for ourselves. I agree with Kathleen Norris: if "being a Christian" means incarnating the love of Christ in my own life, it would be best to let others tell me how well, or how badly, I'm doing.[1]

Besides, I wasn't sure I could wear the label "Christian" and still practice the craft of history of religions—an academic discipline that bills itself as a nontheological, nonnormative collection of descriptive methods for investigating the world's religious traditions. Anyone in my academic trade sees too much in the world's religious traditions that are creative and wonderful to make exclusivist claims about the superiority of one particular religious tradition over another. I still cannot support religious imperialism of this sort. But historians of religions also see much in all religious traditions that seem self-destructive, irrational, exploitive, and irrelevant to contemporary life. So I wasn't sure I could be a Christian and a historian of religions simultaneously. Nor was I sure I wanted to wear any religious label because, trapped in the Cartesian dualism of my discipline's collection of methodologies, I thought doing so would hinder the objectivity of my scholarship.

John had heard me say all this before—during my student days and in written form in some of my earlier publications, and in papers I had read at conferences about the proper methodology for studying religious "phenomena" (meaning what religious people say, believe, and practice) without asserting normative claims about the truth of what religious people say, believe, and practice. Finally, under an escalator in a New Orleans hotel, he had enough of it and ended our conversation by gently saying, "You know, Paul, you're are a Christian. Christian faith is about trusting the truth in whatever dress it wears and following it no matter where it takes you."

The impact of these words didn't hit me right away, but looking back I think they initiated my particular journey into Christian faith, as I

---

1. Norris, *Amazing Grace*, 238.

gradually discovered that faith in Christ is essentially an interior journey that leads us through time—forward and back, seldom in a straight line, most often in spirals. Each of us is moving and changing in relationship to others and to the world, and if one is grasped by Christian faith, to God. As we discover what our interior journeys teach us, we remember; remembering, we discover; and most intently do we discover when our separate journeys converge in the community that is the church.

As it turned out, my training in history of religions became the foundation for my own personal theological journey. The descriptive questions that are the concern of historians of religions and the normative questions pursued by theologians and philosophers are utterly interdependent. So in my later work I wore two methodological hats simultaneously, and still do as I write this book: that of a historian of religions and that of a Lutheran Christian informed by process theology. Then in 1980 I became a participant in Buddhist-Christian dialogue within the context of the Society for Buddhist-Christian Studies. Finally, about ten years ago, I became interested in science-religion dialogue through my association with the Center for Process Studies in Claremont, California, and the Center for Theology and the Natural Sciences (CTNS) in Berkeley, California. What I have learned from my work in Buddhist-Christian dialogue and my personal dialogue with Muslims in my community in the Seattle area, plus my participation in science-religion dialogue is that the two most important tasks for any Christian theologian is to be in dialogue with the world's religious traditions and the natural sciences This claim underlies everything that follows in the chapters of this book.

Chapter 1, "On Theological Reflection at the Boundaries," focuses on the epistemological issues posed by "boundary" or "limit" questions and the resulting experience of cognitive dissonance. The thesis of this chapter is that the interdependence of boundary questions and cognitive dissonance means that knowledge in any field of inquiry is always incomplete and tentative, no matter the degree of truth or profundity. Accordingly, theological reflection, as well as scientific methods are best undertaken guided by constructionist epistemology. Certainly, the goal of theological reflection, in my case in dialogue with the world's religions and the natural sciences, is the increase of knowledge as a means of creatively transforming Christian faith and practice. But if the interdependence of boundary questions and cognitive dissonance is ignored, as tends to be the case with realist epistemologies, theological reflection is cut off at the knees before it begins.

The topic of chapter 2, "That We May Know Each Other," is religious pluralism. Here, I appropriate Imre Lakatos's description of the structure of "progressive scientific research programs" as a means of developing my own history of religions research program based on the metaphysics of Alfred North Whitehead as a means of coherently defending the pluralist theology of world religions assumed by every chapter of this book. That is (to translate aspects of Whitehead's conception of God into my pluralist research program), my thesis is that the Sacred is the source of order and novelty in the universe to which the particular religious traditions of the world refer in their distinctive experiences, teachings, and practices, named differently in by each tradition.

Chapter 3 is "A Christian's Dialogue with the Buddha." Any theologian who takes religious pluralism seriously knows from experience the cognitive dissonance forced on classical Christian doctrines by boundary questions, particularly the burden placed on the doctrine that participation in Christian faith is the sole means of humanity's salvation. This chapter reflects my participation in Buddhist-Christian dialogue since 1980. I am unlike Paul Knitter, who, writing from the background of his experiences as a Roman Catholic, has discovered that he is both a Buddhist and a Catholic Christian.[2] My experiences as a Lutheran have opened me to Buddhist faith and practice in a way that has creatively transformed my experience of Christian faith. While Knitter embraces a dual religious identity, I do not even as I think persons who have left Christian tradition to become Buddhists (or Muslims or Jews) have not made a wrong choice. Nor do I think that persons experiencing a dual religious identity are not in contact with the same reality I name "God" even if they name or understand this reality differently than I.

In chapter 4, "Is This All There Is?" I argue that dialogical engagement with the natural sciences should tell us something important about each, as well as something important about the structures of the universe. The relation between religion and science is a convergence emerging from the similarities they share in common in spite of differences. This convergence happens when both meet as the boundary limits of each discipline. Both science and religion seek to explain how the universe works and how the meaning of the universe works. While the sciences

2. See Knitter, *Without Buddha.*

and religion do not draw identical conclusions, the parallels between them are as striking as their differences. The thesis of this chapter is that science and religion are complementary human ways of understanding the universe's structure of existence; because if it is true that the universe is purposeful and meaningful, as Christian faith affirms, then whatever meaning might exist must be reflected in the physical structures that engage science and religion in general, and science and Christian faith in particular. Science and religion are not rivals.

Chapter 5, "Who Do You Say That I Am?" is a christological reflection. Like the sciences, theological reflection lives at the boundaries of experience and intellect; and, like the words of a good poem or a Zen *koan*, theological reflection points beyond itself to truths that are elusive, that resist words and conceptualizations. This is historically the case with the claim that glues the pluralism of Christian faith and practice together: two thousand years ago human beings encountered God incarnated in the life, death, and resurrection of a Jewish peasant. Certainly not all that God is, but nevertheless God within the conditions of historical existence. Christians have been trying to figure out the meaning of the historical Jesus's question to the Apostle Peter for two thousand years: "Who do you say that I am?" (Mark 8:29). This chapter is about what confessing the historical Jesus as the Christ of faith might mean in the context of contemporary religious pluralism.

Chapter 6 is about "Social Engagement with Unjust Systemic Boundaries." Its thesis is that religious faith and practice do not separate us from the world or each other; faith lived at the boundaries throws us into the world's rough-and-tumble struggle for justice for the human community and the environment. Any theological reflection that does not wrestle with the systemic boundaries that create injustice in the world is as self-serving as it is impotent.

The theme the last chapter, "The Final Boundary," is eschatology, meaning reflection on the final destiny of the cosmos. Eschatology is perhaps the most difficult question for theological reflection because it forces theologians to deal with the fact of death. Death is the ultimate boundary because before we can know anything, we have to first experience what we know as we surround it with verbal description. But by the time we experience *our* deaths, it may be too late to know what we've experienced. Furthermore, if it is confirmed that the universe's expansion continues forever, the universe itself seems condemned to pointlessness, and human existence is merely a brief episode in its history. So the futility of the universe over a time scale of trillions of years is not different from the theological problem this poses for the eventual futility of ourselves over a time scale of tens of years. According to the sciences, death is built into the structure of the universe because of the Second Law of Thermodynamics, which asserts that in isolated systems far from equilibrium because of insulation from external influences, things and events tend to become disorderly. In other words, existence is terminal. This means that cosmic death and the death of human and nonhuman life forms pose equivalent questions about the nature of God's intentions for the universe and its laws, including the Second Law of Thermodynamics. The theological issue is the faithfulness of God and the constant and everlasting seriousness with which God regards all creatures that have lived, now live, or will ever live. This chapter is a reflection on the grounds for trust in the faithfulness of God.

I wish to express my gratitude to the following people who worked to bring this book to fruition. As anyone reading this book will notice, John B. Cobb Jr. in his writings and personal conversations has guided my theological reflections for over forty years. But I cannot claim that I am one of Cobb's students, although I was enrolled in his first seminar on Whitehead's philosophy at the Claremont Graduate University, then known as the Claremont Graduate School. But I have devoured most of what he has written with the appetite of wolves at entrails. It was Cobb who convinced me that I can be a theologian and an historian of religions too. I am now in my seventies, and I am quite surprised that it took me so long to come to this realization.

I also wish to thank K. C. Hanson of Cascade Books for his work in bringing *Theological Reflections at the Boundaries* to publication. I am also grateful to his associates Christian Admonson, Jeremy Funk, and Patrick Harrison for their editorial assistance as well. It is always a pleasure working with such skilled professionals.

Finally, I wish to dedicate *Theological Reflections at the Boundaries* to my grandson, David Christian Kinner: age five and not afraid of boundaries, an inspiration to his grandfather, and a great teacher for his age.

Paul O. Ingram
Mukilteo, Washington

1

On Theological Reflection at the Boundaries

NEWS FROM THE HUBBLE Space Telescope or from a nuclear accelerator or the human genome project will not be scientific proof for the existence of God. Nor do the sciences rule out the existence of God. Seen theologically and coupled with a post-Einsteinian perspective, the universe offers signs of grace because its immense scales macroscopically and microscopically can serve a believer as an icon of the greatness, creativity, and generosity of the God who breaks all boundaries. The God of a universe such as this cannot be a small tribal god. Here the mystics of all religious traditions are in agreement; anyone who thinks that they know what God is, or is not, is either very stupid or in need of a psychiatrist. God is the ultimate mystery, beyond the capture of all imagines, experience, doctrines, languages, or scientific theories. Both scientific theories about physical processes and theological language about God are metaphorical symbols that point to boundaries separating what can reasonably be known from that which transcends what is known. Appropriating a Zen Buddhist metaphor, they are fingers pointing at the moon, but they are not the moon, and it is foolish to identify fingers pointing at the moon with the moon. This is so because scientific descriptions about natural process and theological reflection about God always take place at the boundaries between immanence and transcendence. There are always "boundary" or "limit questions."[1]

In the natural sciences, boundary limits are questions that arise in research that cannot be answered by means of the scientific methods used to describe physical processes. Boundary questions arise because

1. See Ingram, *Buddhist-Christian Dialogue in an Age of Science*, 27–29; Ingram, *The Process of Buddhist-Christian Dialogue*, 134–39; and Ingram, "Constrained by Boundaries," 105–28.

1

(1) scientific methods of investigation are intentionally limited to extremely narrow bits of physical reality while simultaneously ignoring wider bodies of aesthetic, moral, and religious experience, which (2) results in the incompetence of scientific methods to address aesthetic, moral, and religious experience. Furthermore, in agreement with Karl Popper, most working scientists believe that scientific theoretical constructions are intentionally falsifiable. Often, scientific explanations themselves require expanded theoretical explanation.

For example, Isaac Newton's three laws of motion provide a general theory of the gravitational motion of terrestrial objects, such as falling apples and the orbits of planets in our solar system. But Newton was unable to offer a physical theory of gravity itself and was deeply troubled by the notion of "action at a distance," which he believed was intrinsically impossible in a universe governed by a lawful creator deity. So he concluded that God keeps the orbits of planets from changing so that, for example, the moon and the earth do not collide. Albert Einstein's general theory of relativity, while maintaining Newton's three laws of motion, minus Newton's theological commitments, fills this gap in Newton's theory by exploring gravity as the warping of space by objects such as planets, stars, galaxies, and (on Earth) apples falling from trees—rather than action at a distance under the controlling power of God.

This is an example of how a scientific boundary question often creates methodological constraints that often lead to deeper knowledge of the universe's physical structures. Yet in doing so, scientific boundary questions also generate metaphysical questions along with descriptive scientific questions. For example, the "standard model" of big bang cosmology imposes a temporal boundary (13.7 billion years ago) that constrains what we can know about the universe. Why is there a universe at all? The standard response is that cosmologists can describe *how* the universe originated with a high degree of probability after the first three minutes from t=0, but are ignorant about *why* the universe exists. Here, a boundary question generated by the application of scientific methods in physical cosmology creates a metaphysical question that cosmology is incapable of answering. Whenever such scientific boundary questions occur, an opening is created for science-religion dialogue in general, and theological reflection in particular.

Boundary questions are not limited to the natural sciences. Theological questions incapable of solution through the application of theological or philosophical methods arise at the boundaries engendered by what Joseph Campbell called "the universals of human experience," meaning experiences all human beings undergo no matter what their cultural or religious environments might be. For example, the experience of suffering raises the theodicy problem for classical Christian theism. How can a loving, omniscient, omnipotent creator of the universe permit unmerited suffering? Here, the assertion of God's unlimited creative power and unlimited love creates a boundary question that cannot be resolved apart from rethinking the nature of God, as in process theology.[2]

This is so because in science and theology, boundary constraints generate the experience of cognitive dissonance. Which is not to say that boundary constraints with their resulting cognitive dissonances do not imply that reliable knowledge is impossible in the sciences or in theology even as boundary constraints imply that absolutely certain knowledge is impossible. But to conclude that scientists or Christians (or Buddhists, Muslims, or Jews) cannot obtain certain knowledge via scientific methods or the practice of theological reflection does not imply that the sciences have not amassed an incredible body of reliable knowledge about physical reality, or that Christians have not accumulated large bodies of reliable knowledge about the structures of human existence.

Accordingly, we need to understand that knowledge in any field of inquiry is always incomplete and a bit tentative, no matter the degree of truth or profundity. The goal of theological reflection, in my case through dialogue with the world's religions and the natural sciences, is to deepen knowledge as a means of creatively transforming Christian faith and practice. But if the interdependence of boundary questions and cognitive dissonance is ignored, dialogue of any sort is cut off at the knees before it begins.

THE DYNAMICS OF COGNITIVE DISSONANCE

I first encountered the concept of "cognitive dissonance" as an undergraduate philosophy major in the work of Polish microbiologist and historian of science, Ludwik Fleck.[3] More recently, at a conference at

---

2. Cobb, *A Christian Natural Theology*, chap. 5; Cobb and Griffin, *Process Theology*, chap. 3.

3. Fleck, *Genesis and Development of a Scientific Fact*.

St. Anne's College, Oxford University, I encountered an application of Fleck's concept to the science-religion dialogue in the work of intellectual historian Barbara Herrnnstein Smith. She has applied the concept of cognitive dissonance to a number of fields, including literary studies, science-religion dialogue, theology, politics, the sociology of knowledge, and constructivist historical theory and epistemology.[4] Accordingly, the following interpretation of the dynamics of cognitive dissonance is inspired by the work of these two Fleck and Smith.

The experience of cognitive dissonance has several interdependent dimensions. Physically, it is an impression of inescapable noise or acute disorder, a rush of adrenaline, sensations of alarm, a sense of imbalance, chaos, at times feelings of nausea and anxiety. These forms of bodily distress can occur when one's ingrained, taken-for-granted sense of how things are, will be in the future, or *should* be is suddenly confronted by something very much at odds with it. Perceptually, cognitive dissonance may be experienced as a wave of vertigo, for example, at the sight of human disfigurement.

Besides sensory or aesthetic experience, precepts that engender cognitive dissonance can be more or less intellectual, as well as textual. Thus a sense of intolerable wrongness in some politician's description of the issues at stake in an election, or a fellow academic's theoretical description of an issue, can set one's mind on edge and produce a flurry of corrective intellectual activity: letters to the editor, rebuttals, essays, and books. The corrective impulse here is likely to be particularly energetic when one experiences the wrongness as one's responsibility; not, that is, as one's "fault" but as bearing on one's social and professional identity, so that a response seems summoned and obligatory. In all of this, the goal is to end the pain, to get things to "feel right," that is, "back to normal" again.[5]

But exactly how one responds to cognitive dissonance will depend on the various features of the situation itself plus one's own relevant dispositions. Thus while there is no single form of response to an experience of cognitive dissonance, individuals, communities, and cultures possess characteristic styles of response to a perceived anomaly. For example, some people and communities draw ideological boundaries around

4. See Smith, *Belief and Resistance*; Smith, *Scandalous Knowledge*; Smith, *Natural Reflections*.

5. Smith, *Belief and Resistance*, xv and 71–85.

themselves as a prophylactic shield to block out cognitive dissonance, which is the standard strategy of fundamentalism in all its forms. Other communities attempt conversion, while others are prepared to rearrange their worldviews to absorb cognitive "others"; some communities regularly sally forth to slay "the other." This last point entails violence against what is perceived as cognitively other—from domestic abuse and vigilante justice to inquisitions and international crusades that may accompany the attempt to right what ever is perceived to be wrong. As the history of religions demonstrates, particularly in Christian tradition, but also in other religious traditions, the pursuit of normative rightness— truth, health, morality, reason, or justice—at times has its own violent motivations and expressions.

Here lies the relevance of cognitive dissonance for the practice of theological reflection: if what I believe is true, then how can another human being's skepticism of my beliefs be taken seriously? The stability of every belief, every worldview, every religious tradition depends on a stable explanation for resistance to that belief, worldview, or religious tradition, coupled with a coherent account of how beliefs, worldviews, and religious traditions are formed and validated. This is the classic role of apologetic theology in Christian tradition and Buddhism's "philosophy of assimilation," according to which Buddhism incorporated non-Buddhist ideas and practices into itself, even as Buddhism rejected what could not be assimilated in transmitting itself throughout South and East Asia.[6]

According to Smith, there are two "favored solutions" to this puzzle: demonology" and "dementology." By "demonology," she means "the comforting and sometimes automatic conclusion that the other fellow is either a devil or a fool, while "dementology" means that "he or she suffers from defects or deficiencies of character and/or intellect: ignorance, innate incapacity, delusion, poor training, captivity to false doctrine, and do on."[7] Both solutions reflect "epistemic self-privileging" or "epistemic symmetry," meaning the inclination to assert that what we believe to be true corresponds to reality (the way things really are), while other persons believe the foolish things they do because there is something wrong with them.[8] Such epistemologies are "referential" because they

---

6. Matsunaga and Matsunaga, *Foundation* 1: chap. 1.

7. Ibid., xvi. Also see Smith, *Scandalous Knowledge*, 154–55.

8. For a fuller account of this self-standardizing and pathological tendency when

assume congruence between statements and/or beliefs and determinate features of an external reality that are there to be discovered even if no one discovers them.

Consequently, a key concern in current epistemological discussion is the programmatic effort of some philosophers, sociologists, historians of science, and conservative theologians—including many in my own Lutheran tradition—to maintain "symmetry" in their accounts of scientific, political, physical, and theological beliefs and opinions. The epistemological commitment here is the assertion that the *credibility* of all beliefs depends on their correspondence to the actual structures of an objective reality that exists independently of our beliefs or perceptions. This is the epistemological heart of "foundationalism." In its most general terms, foundationalism is the realist or positivist idea that our mistaken beliefs can be corrected by our encounters with an autonomously resistant reality, a current model of which is the popular view many people have of the natural sciences. In foundationalist epistemologies there is little room for interreligious dialogue or science-religion dialogue.

But there is another, more controversial idea, sometimes described as a "hermeneutical circle": that our perceptions and descriptions of the things and experiences we encounter cannot be independent either of our prior beliefs about those things or of our more general presuppositions and verbal/conceptual practices rooted in communal assumptions about what is true and what is false. This is the starting point of constructivist epistemologies. Three points differentiate constructivist epistemologies from foundationalist or "realist" epistemologies.

First, constructivists *do not* characteristically deny *metaphysically* what realists characteristically maintain: that nature *is* structured in certain ways inherently, and that those ways are largely in accord with human perceptions. But constructivists deny that such accounts are fully in accord with the metaphysical structures of nature, because nature always escapes the methodological boundary limits of all academic disciplines and is, because of the resulting cognitive dissonance, always more than we can know. In other words, we are always "constrained" by the "boundary questions" lurking in all academic disciplines. We have partial glimpses, but not complete or certain knowledge in any field of inquiry. This ontological agnosticism is not, as realists might argue, a

---

one experiences cognitive dissonance, see Smith, *Contingencies of Value,* 36–42.

perverse refusal of common sense or a descent into debilitating relativism, but an effort at methodological modesty and theoretical economy.

Second, metaphysically and epistemologically constructivists are typically nominalists. Classically, "nominalism" is the view that universals are names given to particulars sharing common perceived qualities. But constructivist nominalism assumes as crucial the role of active, ongoing acknowledgment of the theoretical significance of language in the construction of knowledge. That is, in constructivist accounts of knowledge, nominalism expresses itself as the ongoing questioning of the standard meanings of such terms as *fact, discovery, evidence, proof, objectivity,* and, of course, *knowledge.*

Which means, third, such terms and concepts operate as elements of larger systems or networks of assumptions, beliefs, and discursive practices that are internally interconnected and, for that reason, powerfully normative. This is why terms like *planet, element, organ, disease, race, gene,* or *intelligence*—and similarly, *knowledge, science, reason,* or *reality*—are understood by Fleck and Thomas Kuhn as having meaning, not in individual and fixed relations to particular objective referents, but as parts of historically and culturally specific systems of beliefs and practices. In this regard, Smith emphasizes three points: (1) the interrelatedness and high degree of mutual determination of *conceptual-discursive elements* (ideas, definitions, distinctions, predictions), *perceptual-cognitive dispositions* (observations, classifications, interpretations), and *material practices* (measurements, manipulations, design and manufacture of instruments; (2) the social construction and maintenance of elements of these systems: that is, the cognitive, social, and pragmatic interactions among particular communities; and (3) the resulting *contingency* of the epistemic viability of the systems and their elements: notably the dependence of the specific meaning and force of individual terms and concepts within specific communities.[9]

Since the 1960s the constructivist views outlined above have been wrongly interpreted by—and criticized as implying—an everything-is-equally-valid relativism, so that anything goes in the practice of science, theology, or any other academic discipline. In fact, no constructivist thinker is a relativist in this sense, even as they presume that knowledge and belief are relative to the social, political economic, and cultural context of the knower or the believer. But what these views *do* imply

9. Smith, *Scandalous Knowledge*, 6–8.

is the conceptual and empirical inadequacy of prevailing "realist" or "objectivist" accounts of method, theoretical construction, and truth because as Flick and Smith point out, all beliefs and worldviews—including Christian theological systems, and scientific theoretical systems—become eventually incoherent and thereby in need of constant revision, a point in harmony with the second-century Buddhist logician, Nagarjuna's "middle way" (*Mādhyamika*).[10] As will become evident, my intellectual sympathies lie with constructivism. But first, four examples of cognitive dissonance will illustrate role of cognitive dissonance in scientific and theological construction.

The Heisenberg Uncertainty Principle

From an evolutionary standpoint, cognitive dissonance, is part of the human condition because it has enhanced the survival of our species. Not always, but often, cognitive dissonance forced our ancestors into new lines of behavior when confronted with unexpected danger in their environments, either from other animals, human groups, or new ideas. Cognitive dissonance continues to be the primary force energizing progress in human culture and ideas that are foundational to human survival, even as it often engenders negative consequences for human beings and other life forms with whom we share this planet. The following examples—one from science, one from Christianity, one from Buddhism, and one from current science-religion dialogue—can serve as a demonstration of this point.

In the mid to late 1920s a small community of physicists proposed a new mathematical formalism for atomic physics and thereby threw physicists kicking and screaming into cognitive dissonance. By 1927 the sciences' attempts to extract order from confusion about physical reality crashed into an unexpected roadblock. In March of that year, Werner Heisenberg set down a piece of mathematical reasoning that was simple, elegant, and quite startling. At first he struggled to find a word for his discovery and used a German word that translates into English as "inexactness." At other times, he tried "indeterminacy," and finally, under the influence of his teacher, Niels Bohr, grudgingly added a postscript that

---

10. See Streng, *Emptiness*, 155–80.

brought a new word into the vocabulary of physicists: "uncertainty"; his discovery is now called the "uncertainty principle."[11]

Not that Heisenberg introduced uncertainty into science. What he changed was the very nature and meaning of science itself by undermining one of the fundamental assumptions of classical physics. Starting with Copernicus, Galileo, Kepler, and Newton, classical physics evolved through the application of logical reasoning to experimentally gathered data and verifiable objective physical facts. Theories couched in the rigorous language of mathematics were intended to be both analytical and precise, which still remains the goal of science after Heisenberg. Thus in the universe described by physics before Heisenberg, nothing happened unless it was caused by something else. This universe was assumed to be an absolutely mechanistic and deterministic system without spontaneity; natural phenomena might be extremely complicated, but at bottom there is always order and predictability. Facts are facts, laws are laws, and there can be no exceptions.

This vision was the dominant model for physics until 1927. Physicists—and geologists, biologists, and the first generation of psychologists—pictured the natural world in its entirety as in intricate and "inerrant" machine. So the goal of physics was characterized in terms of precise observation of physical phenomena that lent themselves to precise mathematical description, meaning reducible to mathematical relationships, and then finding natural laws that tied those relationships into an inescapable system. This is why Heisenberg's uncertainty principle was so unsettling. It pointed to an unsuspected weakness in the edifice of physics that had never been critically examined because it seemed so self-evidently true, given the reductionist materialism and determinism assumed by most scientists since Galileo's time.

Here's how. How is it possible to acquire knowledge about the world of the sort that can be subject to scientific investigation? How, in the particular direction Heisenberg took, do we know where something is and how fast it is moving? The short answer is, we can't know. You can measure the velocity of a particle, or you can measure its position, but you cannot measure both simultaneously. So the more you find out about a particle's location, the less you know about its velocity; the more

---

11. For good treatments of Heisenberg's Uncertainty Principle and Einstein's negative reaction to it, see Jamner, *Einstein and Religion*, 124–38; see 221–36 for the influence of Spinoza on Einstein's physics. Also see Kindley, *Uncertainty*.

you know about its velocity, the less you know about its location. The act of observation changes the thing being observed; the act of measuring changes the thing being measured. The bottom line is that what previous physicists called "facts" are not the simple hard point-entities scientific materialism posits them to be. Heisenberg seemed to be saying that a physicist cannot always find out what she or he wants to know, that physics' ability to describe the natural world is radically circumscribed.

The implications of the Heisenberg uncertainty principle came on the heels of an equally remarkable, and equally perplexing, insight that he had published two years earlier, when he proposed a theory that is now known as "quantum dynamics." This involved rewriting the fundamental rules of particle physics in a new theoretical language that he never claimed to have fully understood. But his mentor, Niels Bohr, saw the need to assimilate quantum dynamics into Albert Einstein's general theory of relativity. Bohr's goal was to make sense of quantum indeterminacy without overthrowing the successes of classical physics. He argued that "probability" at the quantum level is not "a quantity which casually fixes the effect of an atomic collision in an individual event" so that the question of determinism is "a philosophical question for which physical arguments alone do not set standards."[12]

It was at this point that Einstein entered the argument. By this time, Einstein was close to fifty, an "old man" of science, revered, but not often listened to. In 1905 his special theory of relativity had overthrown the Newtonian idea of absolute space and time. Events that one observer saw as simultaneous might seem to another to happen in sequence, one after another. A third observer might see that sequence reversed. Heisenberg concluded that Einstein's special theory of relativity and his quantum theory of light particles (photons) supported his uncertainty principle. But to Einstein, this was a misinterpretation of one of his greatest achievements.[13]

Of course special relativity theory allowed for different perspectives when observing or measuring physical events. But for Einstein, the whole point of special relativity was that it allowed *apparently* contradictory observations to be reconciled in a way that all observers could accept. In Heisenberg's and Bohr's quantum world, the very idea of a

---

12. Born, *The Bohr-Einstein Letters, with Commentaries*, 90.

13. Isaacson, *Einstein: His Life and Universe*, 324–26; 344–49.

"true fact" seemed to crumble into a multitude of contradictory views.[14] As Bohr explained it, probability is not a matter of experimental error or a mathematical fiction because the laws of nature do not determine the occurrence of an event, but the probability of its occurrence."[15] Einstein disagreed: the "uncertainty" of Heisenberg's principle was epistemological because uncertainty exists in the minds of observers, not in nature. But according to Bohr's "Copenhagen interpretation," which is the position held by most working physics today, uncertainty resides in quantum phenomena as such. Einstein spent the remainder of his life trying to disprove the Copenhagen interpretation because: (1) it contradicted his materialist-deterministic view of nature, a metaphysical viewpoint inspired by the Jewish philosopher Baruch Spinoza;[16] (2) it contradicted his religious views, also inspired by Spinoza, that "God does not play dice with the Universe";[17] and (3) his view that the goal of science is to discover certain truth expressed mathematically about the physical processes at play in nature.[18]

Einstein never recovered from the cognitive dissonance of Bohr's interpretation of Heisenberg's uncertainty principle, and this is the primary reason few physicists paid much attention to his work after 1927. Cognitive dissonance still haunts, as it drives, theoretical physicists to search for ways of unifying how the large-scale realities of the universe appear in special and general relativity theory with how the very small realities of the universe appear in quantum theory; both physical theories are fruitful theoretical paradigms focused on different realms of physical phenomena. In the realm of the very small—the realm of elementary particles—quantum physics based on the uncertainty principle is currently the theoretical perspective of most working physicists. But at the level of the very large—the orbits of planets, the physics that allow people to land on the moon or send probes to Mars, Jupiter, and beyond—Einstein's special and general theories of relativity are the

---

14. See the following quotation attributed to Niels Bohr: "It is wrong to think that the task of physics is to find out how nature is. Physics concerns what we can say *about* nature" (see Petersen, "The Philosophy of Niels Bohr," 12).

15. See Einstein, *Relativity*, 64, 155; and Jammer, *The Conceptual Development of Quantum Mechanics*, chaps. 6–7.

16. Jammer, *Einstein and Religion*, 45–47, 53; Isaacson, *Einstein*, 334–39.

17. Isaacson, *Einstein*, chap. 17.

18. Ibid., chap. 11. Also see Paris, "*Subtle is the Lord—,*" chaps. 25–26.

proper theoretical perspectives. Yet the "hard problem" of physics engendered by the cognitive dissonance between quantum physics and relativity physics remains in the form of a search for a quantum theory of gravity that physicists hope will unite quantum theory and relativity theory into one coherent physical theory, a "theory of everything," or TOE. The current candidate for this unification might be "string theory," with its notion of eleven dimensions, in contrast to the four dimensions assumed by quantum theory and Einstein's theories of relativity.

Nagarjuna and *Śūñyatā*

The experience of cognitive dissonance is well known, if not well understood, in the realm of religious faith and practice, as anyone who has tried to figure out the meaning of a Zen *koan* can attest, or as anyone who has tried to figure out the relation between human freedom and God's all-powerful will and goodness in John Calvin's doctrine of double predestination can attest. Furthermore, cognitive dissonance, as in the sciences, can either hinder or energize creative transformation in a particular religious tradition. In the case of Buddhism, the practice traditions of koan meditation are meant to intentionally generate the experience of cognitive dissonance. The historical foundation of this particular Buddhist practice originates in the epistemology of the second-century Buddhist logician Nagarjuna.

Many Buddhists and Christians writing about Nagarjuna's notion of *śūñyatā* or "Emptying," in my opinion, push this concept to some rather incoherent metaphysical conclusions Nagarjuna would never have accepted. This is so because much Buddhist (and Christian) writing on Emptying lacks reference to the textual context of this notion in Nagarjuna's "Middle Length Sayings" (*Mādhyamika-kārikās*).[19] The trouble lies in the tendency to transmute *śūñyatā* into a metaphysically ultimate reality. As Christopher Ives correctly points out, even Masao Abe's claim that *śūñyatā* is the foundation of all religions transforms an originally epistemological notion into a metaphysical claim about ultimate reality—something Nagarjuna would have rejected.[20]

It is clear that Nagarjuna did not employ the notion of Emptying to establish a "metaview" of any sort. He was not interested in establishing

---

19. The best translation of Nagarjuna's "Middle-length Sayings" (*Mādhyamika-kārikās*) is still Streng, *Emptiness*, 47–57.

20. Ives, "Masao Abe and His Dialogical Mission," 348–53.

a metaphysical viewpoint at all, including a Buddhist one. His point was that all things and events are "empty" of "own-being" (*svābhava*). Since all things and events are empty of "own-being," all things and events are impermanent.

Accordingly if we experience—through meditation—every thing and event as empty of "own-being, including our particular philosophical or religious traditions, we cease clinging to them, because in an impermanent universe, there is nothing to which we *can* cling, including Buddhist ideas about the connection between clinging and suffering. Here emerges a profound cognitive dissonance. When we stop clinging, we cease experiencing life as "unsatisfactory" (*duhkha*). In other words, the import of *śūnyatā* is about not clinging to "views," including Buddhist views, since clinging to ideas and doctrines, even Buddhist ones (and I would add Christian ideas and doctrines) is, in Nagarjuna's opinion, the primary source of human suffering. Or translated into my language, clinging to "views" is the primary source of fundamentalism wherever it occurs. Fundamentalists clinging to their group's doctrinal formulations in all religious traditions have certainly caused much suffering.

Nagarjuna's view of nonclinging to doctrinal formulations, even Buddhist ones, remains an important Buddhist "doctrine"—note the cognitive dissonance—particularly in Zen tradition. This is so because Nagarjuna did not intend *śūnyatā* to be taken as a blanket injunction against the use of language. Even he talked about *śūnyatā*. But his point was that we should not create, and thereby cling to, linguistically constructed doctrinal permanencies in an impermanent universe of processive becoming. In other words, concepts, notions, doctrines, symbols, and practices are at best "secondary truths" or "skillful methods" (*upāya*) that may symbolically point the way toward Awakening—provided we do not falsify reality—meaning the way things really are—into islands of permanency by clinging to notions, doctrines, concepts, and symbols *about* reality. It's the clinging that's the problem, not doctrines and teachings as such. Nagarjuna was a second-century-BCE deconstructionist and, I think, an epistemological constructivist.

So what Nagarjuna was trying to do was prepare people for the practice of meditation. Understanding that all religious teaching, practices, and philosophical viewpoints are "secondary truths" did not imply they are devoid of truth. But cling to a secondary truth, you close yourself off from reality—meaning the way things really are, as opposed to the way we think reality is in terms of the secondary truths to which we cling. But after the experience of Awakening, secondary truths are seen for what they are: symbolic pointers. We should never confuse a symbol for the reality to which it points, even if, as Paul Tillich said, symbols "participate" in the reality to which they point. Or stated in another way, Nagarjuna was what Ian Barbour calls a "critical realist."[21] Or to paraphrase a well-known Zen saying, "Before I experienced Awakening, mountains were mountains, trees were trees, and rivers were rivers. When I began my meditative training, mountains weren't mountains, trees weren't trees, and rivers weren't rivers. But after I attained Awakening, mountains became mountains, trees became trees, and rivers became rivers."

GOD AS IMPASSIVELY LOVING

Cognitive dissonance is rampant in the history of Christian theological reflection. Examples abound:

- St. Paul's understanding of faith as freedom from the legal obligations of Judaism, which was quite unsettling to Jewish Christians, particularly the Apostle Peter

- Augustine's doctrine of God's predestinating decision, before the creation of the world, about those persons elected for salvation and those justly headed for damnation as a punishment for original sin; and Pelagius's counterargument that the fall damaged humanity's freedom to choose the good but did not eliminate humanity's freedom to respond to God's grace, for otherwise God is responsible for the reality of sin as well as the existence of evil

- The Nicene Creed's declaration that God's substance (the "stuff" that makes God "God") and humanity's substance (the "stuff" that makes human beings "human") are embodied in the historical Jesus "without confusion"

- Martin Luther's restatement of St. Paul's and St. Augustine's doctrine of justification by grace through faith alone, which caused much cognitive dissonance for many Roman Catholics of his day— and after—since it undercut the need for the Catholic sacramental

---

21. Barbour, *Religion and Science*, 106–10.

system and the need for clergy to mediate God's grace to ordinary Christians.

The list goes on. So for purposes of illustration, I shall briefly focus on the cognitive dissonance inherent in classical theology's reflection on the relation between God's impassivity and God's nature as love. The New Testament and subsequent Christian theology holds that the fundamental character of God is best described by the term *love*. But the meaning of the statement "God is love" is not always clear in classical Christian theism. We know from our own experience that love involves sympathetic response to the persons we love. *Sympathy* means feeling the feelings others, grieving with the grief of others, rejoicing with the joys of others. Nevertheless, traditional Christian theism posits that God's character is identified not only as love but also as completely impassive, which creates a serious cognitive dissonance that has haunted classical theism since the fourth century: classical Christian theism posited a completely impassive deity without sympathetic response toward the creatures of the world that God is declared to love.

In fact, there was always an awareness that divine impassivity, which originates in Greek philosophy, particularly in Aristotle's *Metaphysics*, was in serious tension with the New Testament's notion of divine love for the world. For example, in a prayer of Anselm in the eleventh century, he asks: "Although it is better for thee . . . to be compassionate, passionless, than not to be these things; how art thou . . . compassionate, and, at the same time, passionless?" Anselm tried to resolve this tension by affirming, "Thou art compassionate in terms of thy being"[22] In other words, God only *seems to us* to be compassionate, but God is not *really* compassionate. In the thirteenth century, Thomas Aquinas in the *Summa Theologica* also concluded love is not part of God's nature: "For in God there are no passions. Now love is a passion. Therefore, love is not in God's nature."[23] Thomas then makes a distinction between two kinds of love, one that involves passion and one that does not, after which he concludes, following Aristotle, that God "loves without passion"[24]—similar to the way a physician cures a patient's illness without being affected

22. Anselm, *Proslogium*, 11, 13; cited in Cobb and Griffin, *Process Theology*, 44–45.

23. Aquinas, *Summa Theologica* I, Q, 20, art. 1, obj. 1, cited in Cobb and Griffin, *Process Theology*, 44–45.

24. Aquinas, *Summa Theologica*, ans. 1, cited in Cobb and Griffin, *Process Theology*, 44–45.

by the pain the patient suffers. Accordingly, for Anselm, Aquinas, and subsequent Catholic and Protestant theologians, the model of God at work is that of a father who has no feeling for his children. God does not feel their "experience" or needs, but "loves" them in the sense that God dispassionately gives them good things, which is the meaning of Aquinas's assertion that divine "love" is a purely outgoing sense of "active good will."

The notion of love as purely impersonal and creative is in serious contradiction to the New Testament's teaching that God's love is impartially directed to all creation (God's love, like rain, falls on the just and the unjust) and classical theism's notion that all persons are not equal in regard to God's loving concern, since the majority of human beings are judged by God (because of original sin) to be worthy of eternal torment. Particularly in Protestant theology, but also Catholic theology, love is often defined as "active good will." The idea of sympathetic compassion is missing. In fact, a major contemporary Protestant theological treatise on *agape* ("love") portrays love as totally predestined, with no element of responsiveness on God's part to the experiences of the object of God's love.[25] The implication is that God loves some human beings (a minority of Christians) more than others (the majority of Christians and all non-Christians). In this way, among others, classical theism's notion of divine impassibility undercuts the biblical witness to the love of God.

Process theology has responded to the cognitive dissonance created by classical theology's assertion of divine impassibility in light of the New Testament's quite clear affirmation that God's *is* love actively engaged with the suffering and joys of the world. God in the New Testament is portrayed as anything but impassive. Process theology is often called "dipolar theology," in contrast with classical theology's assertion of divine simplicity. Charles Hartshorne argued that there are two "poles" or aspects of God's nature: God's unchanging abstract essence, what constitutes God eternally as God, and God's concrete actuality, meaning that aspect of God's nature that is temporal, relative, dependent, and constantly changing because of God's relationships with the world. In each moment of God's experiences there are new and unforeseen happenings, which God can experience and know only as they happen. There is no divine predestination, which means that God's concrete knowledge does not include future events before they occur because God's concrete

25. Nygren, *Agape and Eros*, 77–78.

knowledge of the world is dependent on the decisions made by human and other living beings. God's knowledge is always relativized by, in the sense of internally related to, events in the world, indeed the universe itself, as they happen.[26]

Hartshorne's way of conceiving divine dipolarity was influenced by Alfred North Whitehead, but it is not identical with Whitehead's philosophy. Whitehead distinguished between God's Primordial Nature (what God is eternally as God) and God's Consequent Nature (what God becomes through God's continual interaction with all entities in the world at every moment of space-time). God's Consequent Nature is what God becomes from moment to moment as God compassionately interacts with all things and events. In other words, God is fully actual, responsive, and receptive to the ever-changing condition of human and nonhuman beings. Furthermore, this divine relativity is not limited to mere *knowledge of* events in the world. Divine relativity is *responsive sympathy* not only to human beings but also to all entities in existence; it is not merely the content of God's knowledge that is dependent, but also God's own emotional states. In other words, God enjoys our enjoyments and suffers with our suffering.[27] Which, as it turns out, is exactly the way God is portrayed in the Tanakh (wrongly called the Old Testament) and the New Testament.

JOHN F. HAUGHT'S GLOSS ON EVOLUTIONARY BIOLOGY

John Haught is one of many Christian theologians engaged in dialogue with the natural sciences who argue that when understood appropriately, key concepts in current scientific accounts of nature can be recognized as congruent with theological ideas interpreted in relation to these concepts. Haught's dialogue with the natural sciences is primarily with evolutionary biology, and his body of work is among the science-religion dialogue's most important contributions. For Haught, evolutionary descriptions of the origin of life as "spontaneous" (in the sense that the combination of chemicals that gave rise to life was "novel"), coupled with the fact that the genetic mutations driving natural selection are random, can be read to suggest that the laws of nature (taken by Haught

---

26. Hartshorne, *Divine Relativity*, chaps. 2–3; Hartshorne, *Omnipotence*, chaps. 1–2.

27. Whitehead, *Process and Reality*, 342–51.

to entail strict regularity and predictability) leave room for nonnatural agencies, operations, or states.

This "reading" of evolutionary theory is the thesis of his *Deeper Than Darwin*, where Haught develops the idea that biological evolution constitutes a "narrative" or "story."[28] In his words:

> Nature has revealed itself . . . as being an immense story . . . And this story, in turn, may very well be open to many levels of reading. To be perfectly clear here, Darwinism *presupposes*—since by itself it cannot account for—the narrative cosmic tablet on which the life story becomes inscribed. Or, to put it in other terms, our three background ingredients [that is, "contingency," "invariance," and "deep time"] must be waiting on the cosmic table long before Darwinian processes begin mixing and cooking them . . . Neither Darwinism science nor any of the other sciences can satisfactorily tell us "why" nature is constituted in just such a way as to allow the universe to unfold narratively . . . The question . . . invites theological comment . . . [It] could be thought of . . . as purely accidental . . . [But the question is] why any story at all?[29]

Two features are worth noting. First is the joining of expressions of intellectual tentativeness ("[It] could be thought of as . . . purely accidental") with what are portrayed as logical, ontological, or psychological necessities ("Darwin presupposes," "must be waiting on the cosmic table"). Second is the weaving together of the relatively neutral, descriptive language of science ("evolution," "Darwinian process," "nature is constituted") with the metaphoric language of a Christian worldview ("Nature has revealed itself," "cosmic tablet," "the life story becomes inscribed"). Taken together, these features create a sense of combined scientific seriousness, objective necessity, and poetic resonance to an account that might otherwise be seen as a series of gratuitous inferences tenuously strung together: evolutionary biology and the Christian doctrines of creation and redemption are in "consonance." Haught takes this "consonance" as a sign of God's hand in the creation of both the universe and the brains of creatures like us, who learn to read these signs of consonance.

But Haught's notion of consonance also gives rise to cognitive dissonance. His reading of evolutionary theory will be cognitively satisfy-

---

28. Haught, *Deeper Than Darwin*, 23–25.
29. Ibid., 60–62.

ing to those willing to accept it. These are largely people, including me, for whom the major elements and idioms of Christian faith and practice are familiar and who live their lives guided by these idioms. Conversely, those who read *Deeper Than Darwin* not so primed, who operate every day with different beliefs and idioms, will find this notion of consonance not—or not necessarily—wrong or foolish but *gratuitous*: a source not of ultimate meanings revealed but of possible interpretations ingeniously constructed. Nothing in nature or logic can prevent anyone from giving a theological gloss to the findings and concepts of the natural sciences. But, equally, nothing in nature or logic requires anyone to accept them. Theological readings of any natural science remain optional, the product of imaginative possibility, not necessity.

IMPLICATIONS FOR THEOLOGICAL REFLECTION

Given the existence of boundary questions inherent in all methodologies intended to generate real knowledge in all fields of inquiry, and the dynamics of cognitive dissonance inherent in all beliefs and truth claims, particularly in those generated by referential epistemologies, but also by constructivist epistemologies, important implications arise for the practice of theological reflection in dialogue with the world's religions and with the natural sciences.

First, constructivist epistemologies seem to provide a firmer foundation for the practice of theological reflection than referential epistemologies do. My claim here is not that constructivism is free from cognitive dissonance or that it is even desirable or possible that any belief, truth claim, or religious tradition *could* be free from cognitive dissonance. Indeed, this would not be desirable even if it were possible, since a positive function of cognitive dissonance is that it often generates new knowledge.

Examples abound: the changes in physics that occurred after Einstein published his special and general theories of relativity; deeper knowledge of the microphysical realm of physical reality because of Bohr's and Heisenberg's work in quantum physics; the current ongoing search by theoretical physicists to unify Einstein's general theory of relativity with a quantum theory of gravity, a search for a "theory of everything" or TOE; John Cobb's appropriation of the Mahayana Buddhist notion of Emptying (*śūñyatā*) as a means of challenging traditional Christian substantialist notions of God, Christ, and human nature—

all of which are contrary to the New Testament;[30] Cobb's Buddhist dialogical partner, Masao Abe, who appropriated Christian traditions of social activism in the hope of revitalizing Buddhist social activist traditions, now referred to as "social engagement."[31]

In all fields of inquiry, boundary constraints and cognitive dissonance drive the search for new knowledge and understanding. It is also the foundation of dialogue because in all domains of knowledge "we see through a glass darkly." Which does not imply that human beings in all cultures have not amassed incredible bodies of knowledge. But nothing human beings know bears the labels "certain" or "complete." For this reason alone, any dialogue guided by objectivist referential truth claims undercuts dialogue before it can begin, thereby making creative transformation through dialogue impossible.

Second, if what I have described is true (of course not in a referential sense), then the practice of any sort of theological reflection should be based on constructivist assumptions. By *constructivism* I mean, first, a particular way of understanding the relation between what we call knowledge and what we experience as reality ("the way things really are"), so that, second, constructivist accounts of cognition, truth, science, religion, and other fields of inquiry conceive the specific features of what we experience and think about as "the world" (objects, entity boundaries, properties, categories) not as prior to or independent of our sensory, perceptual, and conceptual activities but as emerging from— that is, as "constructed by"—these activities.[32]

Third, constructivist accounts of cognitive processes, including cognitive dissonance and boundary questions, understand beliefs, not as particular correct-or-incorrect propositions about mental representations of the world, but as linked perceptual dispositions and behavioral routines continuously strengthened, weakened, and reconfigured through continual interaction with the cultural, social, economic, educational, historical, and religious environments in which we live. This epistemological view is the opposite of Cartesian-like referential epistemologies that conceive knowledge as a match between statements of belief about matters of fact and objective features located in an exter-

---

30. Cobb, *Christ in a Pluralistic Age*, chap. 13.

31. Abe and Cobb, with Long, "Buddhist-Christian Dialogue," 13–29; and Abe, "God, Emptiness, and Ethics, 53–60.

32. See Smith, *Scandalous Knowledge*, 3.

nal world. For constructivist accounts, truth is a "situation of relatively stable and effective mutual coordination among socially constructed statements, beliefs, experiences, and practical values."[33]

In other words, constructivism is a form of nominalism because it understands knowledge as beliefs that have become relatively well established within particular social and cultural environments. Knowledge and beliefs, like new species of life evolving from previous species in evolutionary theory, emerge from at least three interdependent sets of forces: (1) individual perceptual and behavioral activities and experiences, (2) general cognitive processes originating in the brain's biological structure, and (3) particular social or collective systems of thought and procedure. In this way, knowledge and its accompanying systems of beliefs are "contingently shaped and multiply constrained."[34]

It must again be noted that constructivist epistemologies *do not* deny that there is an external reality existing "out there" beyond the subjective mental processes occurring in the brain. Instead, the specific features of our interactions with reality *are not* prior to and independent of these subjective mental processes but emerge and acquire their specific meanings *through* them. This is why there exists no particular method that characterizes "scientific method" or "theological method" or ("method" in another field of inquiry), because (1) the activities of scientists, theologians, and philosophers are pluralistic; and (2) because these activities always include much that foundationalists view as "unscientific or "nontheological," i.e., biological, social, political, economic, and historical efforts and contexts.

Finally, participants in any dialogue or a Buddhist-Christian-science trialogue should assume, until overwhelming evidence comes to light, that conflicting and apparently incommensurable beliefs, theories, practices, or theories can *profitably affect* each other without having to maintain that one, and only one, set of beliefs, theories, practices, or theoretical perspectives must be, or could be, in the realist sense, correct.

Stated more simply, one can maintain his or her scientific or religious identity without having to assume that the religious identities held faithfully by others do not correspond with objective reality. One need not think of evolutionary biology or Buddhist nontheism as false in order to be a Christian; neither does a Buddhist need to assume Christian

33. Ibid., 4.
34. Ibid., 11.

theism is false to be a Buddhist. Nor need a scientist conclude that all religious traditions are the collective illusions of the scientifically ignorant, as Oxford biologist Richard Dawkins declares. One *can* be a "Christian and a Buddhist, too," as John Cobb has written, provided one is careful to specify what this means.[35] Presumably this holds for Buddhists as well, but this is not something about which a Christian in dialogue with Buddhism can coherently theorize. Still, it is coherent, as some persons have, to assume a multiple religious identity, as exemplified by Roger Corless, who was a Dominican oblate and a practicing Vajrayana Buddhist; and Ruben Habito, who is a Jesuit-trained Christian certified by his Zen teacher, Yamada Kuon Rohi (1907–1989) as his "dharma heir." Finally, one can be a Buddhist or a Christian or both, and a scientist too. It is the experience of cognitive dissonance engendered by the encounter with boundary questions in the practice of dialogue that pushed Cobb, Abe, Corless, Habito, and theologian-scientists like Ian Barbour, Robert John Russell, and Nobel Prize-winning physicist Charles Townes, and others, to the experience of creative transformation of the sort that is blocked by the assumptions of realist epistemologies.

CONCLUSIONS IN PROCESS

As Buddhists generally conclude that the sciences pose few challenges to Buddhist teaching and practice, so many Christian theologians realistically acknowledge the challenges the sciences pose to Christian thought and practice, particularly to Christian understanding of creation and divine action. In its most general terms, what Christian dialogue with the natural sciences has clarified is that if God is anywhere to be known, it will be as God "comes through" in the space-time, physical realities relative to our local existence, since according to the Prologue to the Gospel of John, God is incarnate locally.

This means that God is in relationships because God and nature seem to share this much in common: each must somehow exist with real, objective attributes. But we have no direct access to either God's or nature's attributes except relatively as each is translated into local terms we can understand that can be stretched to grasp something more ultimate than we find in ordinary experience. Certainly the atheistic convictions of scientific materialists that only nature, not God, exists may be correct.

---

35. Cobb, "Can a Christian Be a Buddhist, Too?" 1–20.

But the boundary questions and resulting epistemological problems are the same for atheists, Christian theists, Buddhist nontheists, and scientists: questions that derive from knowing something that transcends our experience and understanding. That the sciences have understood nature, however partially, should be encouragement that Christian theology can deepen its understanding of God and God's interaction with the universe locally, however partial this understanding might be.

Like many theological conclusions, many scientific conclusions are not observer dependent. Scientific conclusions and laws are invariant and do not depend upon a reference frame, even as detailed observations vary from reference frame to reference frame. Some of the physical constants of nature—the speed of light, the charge of an electron, the number of atomic shells, the periodic table, chemical reactions, and so on—will be the same for all observers everywhere, as far as anyone at present knows. Although measurements of space and time are relative to observers, many space-time measurements, which fuse the particulars of space and time in local places, are invariant between observers. There also exists considerable unity in the sciences: mass is unified with energy, space with time, and gravity with acceleration. The very relativity of these interrelationships unifies them, and objectively so. These features of nature remain quite real as phenomena even though they are interdependent with other phenomena. They do not exist intrinsically, but only interdependently—a point that is in harmony with Buddhism's worldview and with Christian process theology.

This is why Christians engaged in dialogue with the natural sciences usually conclude that Christian theological reflection can be harmonized with scientific conclusions about physical processes. Physics and biology have removed nature from the phenomenal level of what human beings experience to a transphenomenal level, where nature is not visible but only detectable. Nature is not unambiguously available to the imaginations of either scientists or theologians or Buddhist philosophers. Nature is rooted in a realm out of immediate reach and only half translated in our phenomenal experience, a region into which we gain access by groping out of our familiar experience.

But since nature is already transphenomenal, why should it be judged incoherent when Christian theologians speak of God in a supraphenomenal way? Scientists, Buddhists, and Christians can stipulate only that they work back from relevant experiences on the phenomenal level and then ask what hypothetical reality might constructively explain these experiences. This is the practice of critical realism as inference to the best explanation. For scientific, Buddhist, and Christian accounts of reality, what can be clearly apprehended stretches away to what we dimly apprehend to what cannot be pictured at all.

In other words, scientific theory and practice and Buddhist and Christian faith and practice are lived at conceptual and experiential boundaries. To cite one example, think of how Christian theological reflection and Buddhist doctrinal reflection can be creatively transformed by a trialogue with the neurosciences. When taken nonreductively, the neurosciences offer explanations of patterns of religious thought and behavior in terms of the interactions between cognitive processes occurring in the brain, contextualized by environmental factors. This is so because neuroscientific accounts of religious experience and behavior inform us that just as culture does not hover above cognition, so cognition is not somehow isolated from culture. Certain conditions of our social and physical environments are broadly similar in all human populations and throughout much of human history, and activate and tune the physical processes generating cognition in similar ways cross-culturally. The similarities of teachings and experience that occur in humanity's religious traditions may be in part explained in terms of the activation and tuning of species-typical cognitive capacities by regular features of the environment. The considerable differences between humanity's religious traditions—the localized features peculiar to all religious traditions—are potentially explainable in the same way.

By investigating the myriad, complex, and variable interactions among brain, mind, body, and environment, the neurosciences offer testable hypotheses concerning particular forms of beliefs in God, nontheism, meditative practices, rituals, complex theologies, and doctrinal traditions across cultures and religious traditions. These testable hypotheses offer opportunities for deepening Buddhist doctrinal reflection and experience and Christian theological reflection and experience. But neither Buddhist nor Christian experience and ways of knowing can be "reduced" to the neuroscientific conclusions about brain states. There are always boundaries.

This is of course, the most important lesson we learn from the interior dialogue between Christian apophatic mystical experience and what our Buddhist brothers and sisters tell us about the experience of Awakening and the emptiness of all conceptual discourse about Awakening, even Buddhist discourse. As Tom Christenson, who teaches philosophy at Capital University, writes, "Some people suppose that talk about transcendence is talk about the supernatural. This is not the way I want to use the term. Something is transcendent if it goes beyond ourselves, for example, if it calls us or demands something from us, or lures us on to a new level of seeing, understanding, or being."[36]

Then Christenson cites one of my favorite hymns in the Lutheran liturgical tradition that is based on the Twenty-Third Psalm: "Shepherd me, O God, beyond my wants, beyond my fears, from death into life." He notes that it is easy to understand a prayer to fulfill our wants or to avoid our fears. But how can we pray to move beyond out wants and beyond our fears? This is transcendence, when something that does not originate from our wants and fears captures us and stretches us beyond our wants and fears, perhaps even beyond our imagining. "Such an encounter can be an occasion for my growth, my conversion, my death, my rebirth, my arrival as a new person."[37]

As Christenson notes, a story can do this. So can insights into the physical process at play in the universe do this. Dialogically encountering another person can do this. Christian experience of God's presence through centering prayer or the Eucharist can to this. Buddhist experience of Awakening can do this. Engaging in Buddhist-Christian conceptual, socially engaged, and interior dialogue can do this. Engaging in a Buddhist-Christian-science trialogue can do this. The experience of transcendence has multiple particular forms, but each throws us out of the conventional limits of our knowledge and linguistic constructs, into boundary constraints that expand our experiences into new possibilities never previously imagined or encountered.

So given the boundary constraints of human knowledge, can anything really be said? In an important sense, the answer is yes, because a great deal has been said and written by scientists, Buddhists, and Christians. Indeed, everything I have written in this chapter is an attempt to contribute to what has been said and what may be said. But can things be said about ultimate transcendence clearly and unequivocally? The lesson of the natural sciences and Buddhist-Christian interior dialogue is, no. This is why as a Lutheran Christian engaged with process

36. Christenson, "The Oddest Word," 179–80.

37. Ibid.

theology I have come to understand that conceptual, socially engaged, interior and science-religion dialogue is the proper form of meaningful theological reflection in a culturally and religiously plural world that is always undergoing process.

So should a Lutheran Christian engaged in dialogue with Buddhists and the natural sciences remain conceptually silent? Perhaps the best answer is, probably more than I do. When scientists, Buddhists, and Christians do engage in dialogical conversation, we should speak and write mindfully, as Buddhist and Christian meditative experience informs us, aware of the temptations involved in trying not to speak or in speaking too much. Again, following the instruction of Buddhist and Christian contemplatives, in speaking about things that reflect transcendence we need to speak and write in an intentionally impaired language by using words that cannot be uttered, in language with a deliberately warped grammar of unsaying, words that always carry a warning: the words we speak or write are not final words. N. T. Wright puts it this way: "All experience is interpreted experience, but not all experience can be reduced to the terms of the interpretation."[38]

38. Wright, *The Resurrection*, 378.

2

"That We May Know Each Other"[1]

BOUNDARY QUESTIONS THAT CREATE cognitive dissonance are experientially clear to Christian theologians dialogically engaged with the world religions and the natural sciences. When an African American imam named Siraj Wahaj served as the first Muslim "Chaplain of the Day" in the Unites States House of Representatives on June 25, 1991, he offered the following prayer, the first Muslim prayer in the history of the House of Representatives: "In the name of God, Most Gracious, Most merciful. Praise belongs to thee alone; O God, Lord and Creator of all the worlds. Praise belongs to Thee Who shaped us as and colored us in the wombs of our mothers; colored us black and white, brown, red, and yellow. Praise belongs to Thee who created us from males and females and made us into nations and tribes that we may know each other."[2]

Siraj Wahaj's prayer is a direct reference to one of the most cited verses of the Qur'an: "Do you not know, O people, that I have made you into tribes and nations that you may know each other." Of course, "knowing each other" is an important goal in the practice of interreligious dialogue and requires breaching social, ethnic, gender, and religious boundaries. But Muslims often move on to cite further Qur'anic advice about religious pluralism: "If God had so willed, He would have made you a single people, but His plan is to test you in what He hath given you; so strive as in a race in all virtues."[3] According to imam Wahaj

---

1. This chapter is a slight revision of chap. 1 of Ingram, *The Process of Buddhist-Christian Dialogue*. An earlier version also appeared in Ingram, "'That We May Know Each Other,'" 135–57.

2. *American Muslim Council Report* (Summer 1991), cited in Eck, *A New Religious America*, 32.

3. Surah 5.51, A. Yasuf Ali, trans.

and the vast majority of Muslims, Islam and pluralism go hand in hand with respect for the dignity of each person no matter what religious or secular label he or she wears. Of course, this interpretation of the Qur'an is rejected by minority radical communities within the House of Islam as well as by fundamentalist communities within Christian, Buddhist, Hindu, and Jewish tradition. Nor are the foundations of pluralism found only in the Qur'an. Buddhist, Jewish, Hindu, and Christian tradition supports religious pluralism as well.

In chapter 1, I tried to specify the epistemological conclusions that underpin my particular theological reflections by focusing on boundary questions and the dynamics of cognitive dissonance. My intention of chapter 2 is to specify the philosophical foundations for the theological reflections in the following chapters of this book. My thesis is that what John Hick calls the "pluralist hypothesis" offers us the most coherent theoretical framework—minus Hick's Kantian epistemology—from which to interpret contemporary postmodern experience of religious diversity. I shall also argue that the pluralist hypothesis constitutes a coherent history-of-religions research program from which to investigate and interpret the facts of religious diversity.[4] As a means of demonstrating the coherency of my thesis and its supporting arguments, I shall appropriate the philosopher of science, Imre Lakatos's account of the methodology and structure of scientific research programs, guided by Nancey Murphy's application of Lakatos's work in the construction of theological research programs. But first, some preliminary clarifications about what I mean by *pluralism* and *diversity*.

THE STRUCTURE OF THE EXPERIENCE
OF RELIGIOUS PLURALISM

Pluralism is not just another name for *diversity*. *Diversity* names the fact of the existence of differing religious traditions among human beings. *Pluralism* goes beyond mere diversity to active engagement with religious plurality. Religious diversity is an observable fact all over the world, but perhaps most observable in America. But without engage-

---

4. While I accept most of Hick's arguments in support of the pluralist hypothesis, I do not assume the Kantian epistemological foundations of Hick's account of religious pluralism. See Hick, *An Interpretation of Religion* chap. 14. What follows in this chapter will be written from the perspective of one convinced of the truth of Whiteheadian process metaphysics and epistemology.

ment with one another, the mere facts of the existence of neighboring churches, temples, and mosques are just salad-bowl examples of diversity. We can study diversity, celebrate it, or complain about it, but diversity alone is not pluralism. This is so because pluralism is not an empirical fact, as religious diversity is an empirical fact. Pluralism is an attitude, a theological orientation, a theoretical construct that seeks to coherently interpret and understand the data of religious diversity.

As a theoretical construct, pluralism is neither an ideology nor a Western neoliberal scheme nor a debilitating form of relativism.[5] Pluralism is best understood as a dynamic process through which we dialogically engage with one another through our very deepest differences. I shall appropriate the metaphysics of Whiteheadian process philosophy as a means of conceptualizing pluralism as dynamic process.

Nor is pluralism mere tolerance of the other, but rather an active attempt to understand the other. Although tolerance is a step forward from intolerance, it does not require neighbors to know one another. Tolerance can create a climate of restraint, but not understanding. Tolerance does little to overcome stereotypes and fears that in fact govern the lives of many religious persons when they encounter the religious other. Pluralism is a theological-philosophical move beyond tolerance based on exclusivist and inclusivist theologies of religions toward constructive understanding of what to make of the empirical facts of religious diversity.[6]

Pluralism is not debilitating relativism. It does not displace or eliminate deep religious or secular commitments. Pluralism is the encounter of commitments. Many critics of pluralism persist in linking pluralism with a kind of valueless relativism in which all perspectives are equally compelling and, as a result, equally uncompelling. Pluralism, they contend, undermines commitment to one's own particular faith with its own particular language by watering down particularity in the

---

5. See the collection of essays edited by Gavin D'Costa, *Christian Uniqueness Reconsidered*. Each contributor to this volume, in varying ways, argues that pluralist theologies of religions, besides being ahistorical, are in fact forms of debilitating relativism and Western forms of intellectual imperialism that reduce the diversity of the world's religious traditions to a particular metaphysic, thereby committing what Whitehead called the "fallacy of misplaced concreteness."

6. See my books *Wrestling with the Ox*, chap. 2; and *The Modern Buddhist-Christian Dialogue*, chap. 2, for my critique of contemporary exclusive and inclusive theologies of religious.

interests of universality. I consider this view a distortion of the process of pluralism, because pluralism is engagement with, not abdication of, differences and particularities. While encountering people of other faiths may lead to a less myopic view of one's own faith, pluralism is not premised on a reductive relativism. The focus of pluralism is on significant engagement with real differences.

The language of pluralism is dialogue. Dialogue is vital to the health of a religious community so that we appropriate our faith, not by habit or heritage alone, but by making it our own within the context of conversation with people of other faiths. The goal of dialogue is not mere agreement, but achieving relationship. As the language of pluralism dialogue is the language of engagement, involvement, and participation. Which means pluralism is a never-ending process, the ongoing work of each generation.

IMRE LAKATOS ON SCIENTIFIC RESEARCH PROGRAMS

Imre Lakatos wrote an influential essay about scientific method titled "Falsification and the Methodology of Scientific Research Programs."[7] In this essay, Lakatos described the actual practice of science in terms of competing research paradigms, rather than a historical series of complex competing paradigms, as it was for Thomas Kuhn.[8] Lakatos described some of these research programs as "progressive" and others as "degenerating." A degenerating research program is one whose core theory is "saved" by ad hoc modifications that form a protective belt—face-saving devises or linguistic tricks—meant to protect the core theory from criticism. As Nancey Murphy points out, it is difficult to know what "ad hoc modifications" mean since it is always difficult to propose criteria for determining what these nonscientific face-saving modifications are.[9]

Lakatos was clear, however, on the conditions necessary for a progressive scientific research program. First, each new version of the theory—what he called its core theory and its hypothesis—preserves the unrefuted content of its predecessor: for example, as Einstein's general and special theories of relativity preserved the unrefuted content of Newtonian physics. The function of the core theory is to unify

7. Lakatos, *Criticism and the Growth of Knowledge*, 91–196.

8. Murphy, *Theology in the Age of Scientific Reasoning*, 58–61; Kuhn, *The Structure of Scientific Revolutions*.

9. Murphy, *Theology in the Age of Scientific Reasoning*, 59.

the program by providing a general view of the nature of the entities being investigated. Second, a "protective belt of "hypotheses" that function as lower-level theories supporting the core theory surrounds this theoretical core. Also included here are theories of instrumentation and statements of initial conditions. Third, there must be empirical data that support both the core theory and the hypotheses. When the first and second conditions are met, a scientific theory is said to be "theoretically progressive." When all three conditions are met the research program is "empirically progressive."[10]

Since in the actual practice of the natural sciences deductive reason based on hypotheses make explanation and confirmation symmetrical, the hypotheses nearest the data being researched explain the data, as higher-level hypotheses explain lower-level theories; while the core theory is the ultimate principle for all data. For this reason, Lakatos described the auxiliary hypothesis as a "protective belt," since potentially falsifying data are accounted for by making changes at the level of the auxiliary hypotheses rather than in the core theory, which he called the "hard core" because it cannot be abandoned without abandoning the entire research program. Thus a progressive research program is fundamentally a temporal series of networks of theory, along with supporting data, in which the core theory stays the same but the auxiliary hypotheses change over time to account for new data and the data's relation to the research program's "hard core."

A progressively mature scientific research program also involves what Lakatos called a "positive heuristic," which is a plan for the systematic development of the program so that it can take account of broad arrays of new data. This reflects the recognition of the role of models in contemporary philosophy of science. Scientists employ a wide variety of models—for example, the double helix model of DNA or other mathematical and physical models of various sorts. The function of a positive heuristic is to envision the development of a series of increasingly accurate models of the processes and entities under scientific investigation. For example, the hard core of Isaac Newton's research program consisted of his three laws of motion and the law of gravitation as influence at a distance. The auxiliary hypotheses included initial conditions and applications of the three laws of motion and gravity to specific problems. The positive heuristic included working out increasingly sophisticated

---

10. Ibid., 59–60. Also see Murphy and Ellis, *On the Moral Nature*, 11–13.

explanations for the orbits of planets: first calculations for a one-planet system with the sun as a point-mass, then solutions for more planets.

Lakatos's description of the structure of scientific research programs places high value on coherence, yet is open to two criticisms: (1) the arguments that justify conclusions are circular, since it is a matter of each part of the theory fitting into the other parts; and (2) it is difficult to judge between two competing and equally coherent research programs, which seems to imply a debilitating relativism. In reply to these objections, Lakatos proposed that a progressive research program is one in which a new hypothesis accounts for the anomaly that led to its inclusion in the program, but also allows for the prediction and corroboration of novel facts, meaning facts not to be expected in light of the previous version of the research program. In this way, a progressive research program's factual foundations increase over time, while a degenerating program's empirical content does not increase to keep pace with the increasing proliferation of empirical data.[11] In other words, the justifications for scientific truth grounded in a particular research program are always pragmatic and historical.

Murphy argues that the scientific methodology described by Lakatos can be applied directly to theology as an academic discipline.[12] As one of several examples, she cites Wolfhart Pannenberg's theology, where the "hard core" is his claim that the God of Jesus is the all-determining reality. This is Pannenberg's central theory that guides the development of his entire theological program. Just as in a scientific research program, the positive heuristic of any systematic theology like Pannenberg's is to engender theories ("auxiliary hypothesis") that meet the following conditions: (1) they are faithful to authoritative pronouncements within particular faith communities; (2) they elaborate or spell out the content of the hard core; (3) they do so in a way that relates a community's doctrines to available data (sacred texts, the authoritative teaching of a community evolving over time, the experiences of participants in a community). In the Pannenberg example, the hard core—his insistence on God's relation to all that has been, is, or will be—requires that "data"

11. For a detailed discussion of "novel facts," see Murphy, "Another Look at Novel Facts," 385–88.

12. See Murphy, *Theology in the Age of Scientific Reasoning*, chap. 6, for examples of particular theological research programs as well as an outline of her particular research program.

include not only biblical texts, but facts and theories from all areas of knowledge, including the natural sciences interpreted through the hard core of his research program.

PLURALISM AS A THEOLOGICAL RESEARCH PROGRAM

The simple fact of religious diversity in itself raises no serious theological issues. "It is only when we add what can be called the basic religious conviction that a problem is generated."[13] By "basic religious conviction" Hick means the conviction that our religious beliefs, practices, and experiences are not illusions because they refer to a transcendent reality that he calls "the Real." Whether such convictions are justifiable is one of the central issues of philosophy of religion. But Hick's point is that all religious persons claim that their beliefs and practices bear ontological reference to a transcendent reality, named and experienced differently within the contexts of humanity's various religious traditions. This constitutes the "hard core" of Hick's pluralist hypothesis and my notion of pluralism as a research program.

Most often, the basic religious conviction carries an additional claim: one's particular religious tradition is the most valid response to "the Real" because it bears an ontological correspondence to "the Real" missing from religious traditions other than one's own. But can such claims—which most participants in all religious traditions assert in their distinctive ways—ever be validated? Hick thinks they cannot since the wider religious life of humanity occurs within the boundary limits imposed by historical and cultural experience. That is, we can only experience and judge truth claims from the particular historical and cultural contexts through which experiences are lived and judgments are made. Thus Hick's conclusion: no one can know the Sacred "as such" but only as mediated through the filters of history, tradition, and culture.

It is this philosophical reading, Kantian in its epistemological assumptions, that leads Hick to posit the pluralistic hypothesis. If (1) the basic hypothesis of humanity's religious traditions is the existence of an absolutely transcendent and real reality (the hard core), then (2) all of humanity's religious traditions should be understood as "auxiliary hypotheses," meaning "different ways of experiencing, conceiving, and living in relation to an ultimate divine reality which tran-

---

13. Hick, *God Has Many Names*, 88.

scends all our visions of it."[14] Accordingly, different forms of religious experience that engender different teachings, practices, and images are not necessarily contradictory or competitive in the sense that the truth of one entails the falsehood of the other. In Hick's understanding, all religious traditions reflect encounters with "the Real" within the context of their particular historical and cultural perspectives.

Hick's pluralist hypothesis has been sharply, and perhaps unjustly, criticized for establishing the truth of multiple religious traditions by reducing them to a single common element. But this is not Hick's claim. He understands perfectly well the diversity of truth claims in the world's religions. A Kantian epistemology might allow one to take such an ahistorical position. But Kantian as he is, Hick does not draw this conclusion. The "hard core" of his theory is that the religious traditions of humanity embody historical experience with an "ultimate reality," which he calls "The Real." His auxiliary hypotheses do not reduce the historical complexity of the world's religions to a single common element.

Therefore, my contention is that objections to the pluralist hypothesis can be met by (1) appropriating Lakatos's model of how scientific research programs actually function, and (2) reformulating the pluralist hypothesis through appropriating Whiteheadian process philosophy. The "hard core" of my research program agrees with Hick's: all religious traditions reflect culturally and historically limited experiences of a reality that transcends them all, and that they all seek to describe this reality in their own terms according to their own traditions. But this reality is incredibly complex, and about the teachings of the religious traditions of the world are not identical; the traditions *do not* affirm the same things even though they are referencing the same Sacred reality. Instead, each particular religious tradition expresses truths intended to be universal, but are not the full truth. That is, the specific religions of the world constitute a series of auxiliary hypotheses intended as true accounts of reality—meaning the way things really are, as opposed to the way we want things to be—even though the teachings and practices of the world's religions are often similar, often different, sometimes contradictory, and occasionally complementary in their differences. A negative corollary of this reformulation is that some teachings and practices in all the world's religions might not bear ontological correspondence to reality to which they refer.

14. Hick, *An Interpretation of Religion*, 237.

If what I have described is accurate, the world's religious traditions potentially express truth claims that either complement or contradict each other. This assumes that different religious traditions address aspects of the human condition relative to their particular culture and history, so that attention must be paid to these differences. Thus, for example, Buddhist concepts of Awakening and Christian concepts of salvation are different and express different religious experiences of the Sacred. But by understanding the differences and raising questions in dialogue, Buddhists and Christians can enrich their own understanding of reality.

The primary mode of theological reflection supported by the particular pluralist research program I am proposing is interreligious dialogue, which is portrayed in figure 2.1 below.

Figure 2.1: Model of a Pluralist Research Program

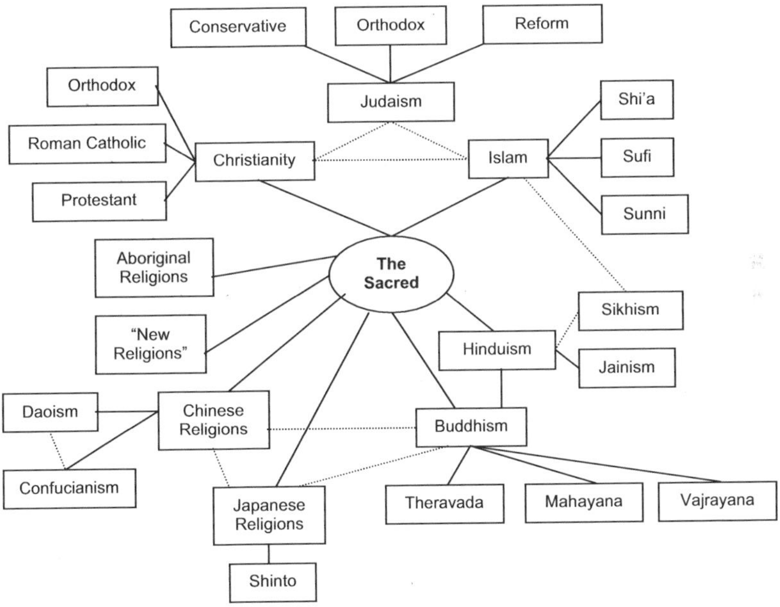

According to Alfred North Whitehead, creativity is "the category of the ultimate," meaning "the universal of universals characterizing ultimate matters of fact" by which "the universe disjunctively becomes the one actual occasion, which is the universe conjunctively." In the process, the "the many become one and are increased by one."[15] As metaphysically ultimate, all things and events (in Whitehead's language, all actual occasions of experience and societies of actual occasions of experience), at every moment of space time—past, present, future—are particular manifestations of this universal creative process, including God, whom Whitehead believed was the chief example of the creative advance. As metaphysically ultimate, creativity has no boundaries, which is symbolized in Figure A by the empty spaces occupied by the circle and the boxes.

The center of the diagram is occupied by a circle upon which I have written "The Sacred"; this refers to what John Hick calls "the Real." Of course, the Sacred is not limited by conventional "boundaries" since, according to Whitehead, God is ingredient in the becoming of all things and events in the creative advance of the universe. My choice of "the Sacred" to designate the central referent in the diagram is a reflection of my training in history of religions, particularly as practiced by Mircea Eliade. Although the term is open to criticism, "the Sacred" seems an appropriate descriptive designation of the referent of religious experience wherever it occurs. Thus while I do intend to employ this term in generic sense in what follows, I also realize that as neutrally as I try to employ it, "the Sacred" carries Western and perhaps even Christian theistic connotations that my not be a fully adequate to the experiences of nontheistic religious persons. Even so, provided one is careful, the term can be employed as a generic designation for the referent of religious experience, practice, and traditions.

While I realize that my interpretation of religious pluralism is open to the foundationalist charge that it posits a "common ground" that often creates a debilitating relativism because it explains by explaining away real religious diversity and difference, persons who make this claim also invest themselves in interreligious dialogue. How this dialogue is possible without reference to a sacred reality that transcends all the particular religious traditions—however it is named—is not often clear. My point is that anyone who practices interreligious dialogue tacitly implies that

---

15. Whitehead, *Process and Reality*, 31–32.

there *is* a common referent to which the collective religious traditions and experiences of humanity point, and it serves no purpose to deny it.[16] This constitutes the "hard core" of my pluralist research program. The specific research problem is how to indicate this common referent more specifically without explaining away the real convergences, incommensurabilities, and diversity that constitute pluralism of the world's religious traditions. An equally important problem of my research program is how to avoid the trap of debilitating relativism.

Returning to figure 2.1, the boxes surrounding the circle bear the names of some of the major religious traditions. I have included the best-known traditions and have left others out (i.e., Zoroastrianism) because I wanted to keep the diagram as simple as possible, yet still to specify the theoretical structure of my research program. In actual practice, one would have to include Zoroastrianism since it is the historical source of Jewish, Christian, and Islamic monotheism. My primary intention is to portray the various religious traditions as "auxiliary hypotheses" that form the "protective belt" surrounding the hard core. Each box is connected to the Sacred by an unbroken line, representing my hypothesis that each of humanity's religious traditions refer to real but historically and culturally bounded experience of the Sacred. The implication is that no particular religious tradition can claim universal validity or absolute truth for all human beings regarding the Sacred to which they all refer.

The broken lines linking Judaism, Christianity, and Islam are meant to indicate that these three monotheistic traditions have shared history, culture, teachings, and practices. The broken lines linking Islam with Sikhism, and Hinduism with Sikhism, represents the origins of Sikh tradition in Guru Nanak's teachings, which sought to harmonize aspects of Islam and Hinduism into a synthesis that could overcome Hindu-Islamic violence. The broken lines linking Chinese Religions and Buddhism, and Chinese Religions and Japanese Religions, indicate the influence of Buddhism in Chinese religious thought and practice in such movements as Neo-Confucianism, as well as to show the influence of Buddhism in the religious history of Japan and its influence on Shinto, and as the primary vehicle by which Confucianism and Daoism were introduced to Japan. The broken line linking Daoism and Confucianism indicates the fact that in the experience of most Chinese persons, Daoist

---

16. For a more complete response to the criticism of "common ground" notions of religious pluralism, see Ingram, *Wrestling with the Ox*, 172–74.

and Confucian tradition do not function as distinct traditions. Finally, the broken line linking Shi'a, Sunni, and Sufi forms of Islam indicate that these three forms of Islam share the defining character of the practice of Islam for all Muslims: the intention to "surrender" to the will of God, but in their own distinctive ways; the broken line here also reflects the fact that Sufism is practiced within both Sunni and Shi'a communities.

The boxes surrounding the major religious traditions represent various subtraditions within each of the major religious traditions. Thus Orthodox, Conservative, and Reform Judaism are themes and variations on three thousand years of Jewish history and experience. Orthodox religious experience, Conservative religious experience, and Reform religious experience constitute the "data" supporting Jewish teaching about the Sacred and its practices. Likewise Orthodox, Roman Catholic, and Protestant forms of Christianity constitute "data" supporting two thousand years Christian experience of the Sacred. Likewise Sunni, Shi'a, and Sufi constitute "data" for the truth and practice of Islamic monotheism. Daoism, Confucianism, and Buddhism are the "data" for Chinese religious experience, while Theravada, Mahayana, and Vajrayana traditions are data for Buddhist teaching and practice.

By "data" I mean the religious experience of persons who participate in the various movements of their religious traditions throughout their histories. Of course, scientific data and the data of religious experience are not identical. For one thing, the data that support scientific theories are public, experimentally repeatable, closely tied to theory expressed mathematically, and are more often than not unrelated to ordinary human experiences of the world. The data of religious experience, while closely related to doctrine and teaching, are not experimentally repeatable, and carry a subjectivity not easily, if ever, open to empirical observation in the way that physical "facts" seem to be in the natural sciences. Nevertheless, the data of religious experience supports the teachings of the various religious traditions as differing referents to the Sacred. Otherwise persons would not be practicing these traditions.

APPLICATION OF THE PROPOSED RESEARCH PROGRAM:
THE HARD CORE

In its application, the pluralist research program I am proposing is not a theological research program because it is not concerned with testing the validity of the specific normative claims or defending a particular religious tradition as the most accurate representation of the Sacred. As Murphy argues, specific theological traditions within Christianity can be viewed as competing interpretations of the hard core of Christian tradition, the incarnation.[17] In this sense, theological research programs tend to be more concerned with normative questions regarding the validity and truth of specific doctrines and practices within a specific religious tradition then the discipline of history of religions, which is focused on more descriptive issues. That is, more or less, theology is typically concerned with, what ought I believe and practice? while history of religions is typically concerned with, what has been believed and practiced by religious human beings no matter where you find them? Of course in actual practice, historians of religions are often involved in normative issues, while theology must establish its normative conclusions on the facts of religious experience revealed by history of religions.

Unlike a theological research, my proposal is a history-of-religions research program that I think has normative implications for the theological and philosophical reflection that occurs in particular religious traditions, but is not itself a means for deciding whether, for example, Pannenberg's theological program is more adequate to Christian experience than Whiteheadian process theology. In fact, I think this is not the case, but I would not apply my pluralist research program to justify the claims of process theology over against Pannenberg. Furthermore, as a Christian historian of religions, I can only try to specify the implications for Christian theological reflection about the most appropriate way to interrelate with the world's religions. A Buddhist, Muslim, Hindu, or Jew accepting this research program would, I suspect, draw different normative conclusions in relating their particular traditions to the world's religions.

I have named the "hard core" of this research program "the Sacred," primarily because I cannot think of another adequate designation. However, what I intend by the designation "the Sacred" is based on my interpretation of Whitehead's conception of God. Three aspects of Whitehead's metaphysics are germane to my proposal. First, as I briefly noted above, is the category of creativity, which Whitehead described as the "universal of universals," meaning that process by which every individual entity in this universe—the "disjunctive diversity" of the

---

17. Murphy, *Theology in an Age of Scientific Reasoning*, 199–207; and Murphy and Ellis, *On the Moral Nature*, chap. 8.

universe—enters into complex unity—the "conjunctive" oneness of the universe. That is, the many actual occasions (all things and events at every moment of space-time) that constitute the disjunctive diversity of the universe become one actual occasion, the universe conjunctively.[18]

This implied for Whitehead that creativity is also the principle of novelty. All things and events are particular, novel entities distinct from every other entity in the universe that the universe experientially unifies. Yet since every actual occasion—every particular thing and event, or societies of things and events—unifies the many that constitutes the universe itself in its own distinctive way according to its particular "subjective aim"; creativity is a process that always introduces novelty into the content of the many things and events that constitute the universe conjunctively.[19]

What this implies is that the creative process at work in the universe has no independent existence apart from the actual things and events undergoing process. Therefore, as "categorically ultimate," all things and events undergo the universal process of creativity, including that actual occasion Whitehead called "God" and which for the purposes of my history-of-religions research program I call the Sacred. That is, all things and events, including God (the Sacred), are concrete instances of the "many becoming one and increased by one."

Second, while all things and events exemplify the process of creativity according to their own "subjective aim," even if only trivially, Whitehead thought that God is the formative element, indeed the chief example of the creative process. Accordingly, Whitehead wrote of God's reality as bipolar, meaning constituted by two interdependent "natures": an eternal unchanging "primordial nature" and a changing, processive "consequent nature." God's primordial nature is God's everlasting self-identity through time; which constitutes God as God, what God always remains. God's "consequent nature" is what God becomes as God affects and is affected by the multiplicity of past and present things and events at every moment of space-time as God unifies all things and events according to God's "subjective aim" that all things and events achieve maximum intensity and harmony of experience.[20] In other words, God's

18. Whitehead, *Process and Reality*, 16, 141; Whitehead, *Science and the Modern World*, 152–53; and Whitehead, *Modes of Thought*, 31.

19. Whitehead, *Process and Reality*, 31–32.

20. Ibid., 531–33.

consequent nature is what God becomes as God experiences and inter-relates with every entity in the universe, while God's primordial nature is an abstraction from the actual process of what God is in God's proces-sive consequent nature. Both natures are interdependent and mutually constitute what God "is" in God's own experience of the universe—and in the universe's experience of God.

Finally, God, according to Whitehead, is the source of novelty and order in existence. The source of novelty is God's primordial envisage-ment of pure possibilities together with an appetition that these possibil-ities be actualized in the universe, which is part of the initial aim given to all actual occasions of experience—which may or may not be taken into account by an occasion's subjective aim. Novelty as an actualiza-tion of new possibilities generally increases the enjoyment of experience because the variety of possibilities that are actualized in the universe add richness, texture, zest, and intensity to both God's and an occasion's experiences. It is this sense that God is the source of novelty. However, there is a connection between order and novelty, which source is also God. Novel possibilities cannot be realized in the universe in simply any order; rather, some novel possibilities become real only after others have been actualized. That is, at one stage certain novel possibilities are realized for the first time, and if they are repeated, they become part of the order of the world that contextualizes the actualization of future novel possibilities, and so on. Thus God is the source of order because (1) order represents the dominance of an ideal possibility that was at one time a novel element in the universe, so that God is the source of order by virtue of being the source of novelty; and (2) neither order nor novelty is intrinsically good, but instrumental to the one intrinsic good, which is the "enjoyment of intense experience." In Whitehead's words, "God's purpose in the creative advance is the evocation of intensities. The evocation of societies [of actual occasions] is purely subsidiary to this absolute end."[21]

Translating the above aspects of Whitehead's conception of God into the pluralist research program I am proposing, the Sacred is the source of order and novelty in the universe to which the particular religious traditions of the world refer in their distinctive experiences, teachings, and practices, named differently in by each tradition. Some religious traditions have emphasized (i.e., "prehended") the nonperson-

---

21. Ibid., 533ff.

al dimensions of the Sacred as ineffable, meaning beyond the ability of language—definition, doctrine, symbols—to fully grasp and conceptually express (e.g., the ineffability of Brahman in Upanishadic Hinduism or "Emptying" (śūñyatā) in Mahayana Buddhism or the Dao (the Way) in Daoist tradition. Included in these examples are mystical traditions such as Sufism and Jewish Kabbalah. Persons who participate in these traditions seek to experience a connection between themselves and the Sacred conceived as nonpersonally transcendent to, yet immanent within, all finite things and events through such disciplines as yoga, meditation, and, in monotheistic tradition, contemplative prayer.

The vast majority of human beings have experienced (i.e., "prehended") the Sacred through a range of specific deities. Judging from the Paleolithic cave paintings in the Grotto of Lascaux in France, experience of the sacred as a personal deity or set of deities with whom one is in relationship probably represents the most archaic expression of religious experience. Yet no one has ever encountered the Sacred as a deity "in general," or for that matter the Sacred as nonpersonal "in general." We never experience anything "in general," but only "in particular," always bounded by historically and culturally situated images and symbols. For as there are different ways of being human and of participating in history, so it is that within the contexts of history and culture the presence of the Sacred as personal (or nonpersonal) is experienced differently.

Christians encounter the Sacred as personal through stories of the life, death, and resurrection of the historical Jesus confessed to be the Christ. Christians in faith trust these stories about the relationship between human beings and God the Father and the Father's continuing work in the world through the Holy Spirit. Similarly, Jews bet their lives on the gift of Yahweh's Torah ("instructions") and the resulting covenant between Jews and their Lord through Moses on Mount Sinai. Muslims surrender their wills ('islām) to Allah, "the God," as recited by the Prophet Mohammed in the Qur'an, "the Book wherein there is no doubt," wherein Muslims believe is recorded the "straight way" of humanity's most complete religion. In Hindu devotional faith, the Sacred is experienced as Siva, Vishnu, Kali, Krishna, Rama—in as many forms of Brahman as you please. Mahayana Buddhists, perhaps the majority, encounter the Dharma beyond name and form masked by a multiplicity of Bodhisattvas. Aboriginal people encounter the Sacred personified in wind, rain, mountains, lakes, rivers, sun, moon, stars, and the natural forces of growth and decay.

Still, there is always something nonpersonal about personalized forms of the Sacred as deities. It is not just that the deities often interrelate with nature and human beings nonpersonally—Jesus is reported to have noticed that like God's rain, God's love for creation is disinterested and falls on the just and the unjust, so don't take it personally. Images of deities also reveal that the Sacred is infinitely beyond the scope of human understanding and cultural and historical perspective. Yet, as both the nontheistic and theistic religious ways of humanity teach, just because we cannon know *everything* about the Sacred does not mean we cannot know *something*, since according to a Whiteheadian version of religious pluralism, the Sacred is always interacting with the particulars of the universe as the source of ordered novelty.[22]

THE AUXILIARY HYPOTHESES:
HUMANITY'S RELIGIOUS TRADITIONS

The central question of my pluralist research program is, how should we understand the facts of religious pluralism and engage in interreligious encounter so that everyone has not only the right to speak but also genuine ability to hear what is spoken? This is not an easy question, but the view I am proposing assumes as a start the existence of a common referent to which all the religious traditions of humanity point in their own historically-culturally contextualized ways. It seems to me that any notion of interreligious dialogue must assume a common referent, sometimes called a common ground, underlying the diversity of humanity's religious experience and history. As a process thinker, I find *common ground* troublesome because this term seems to imply an unchanging substantial "essence," a notion contrary to Whiteheadian metaphysics and the natural sciences. But the religious traditions are in reference to something that each names differently according to particular histories of encounter with this referent. I have chosen to call this referent the Sacred, but several other names for this referent have been proposed: the "common essence" of Arnold Toynbee, the object of "universal faith" posited by Wilfred Cantwell Smith and Bernard Lonergan, the "com-

---

22. For a more developed discussion of experience of the Sacred as nonpersonal and personal, see Ingram, *Wrestling with the Ox*, 76–86.

mon mystical center" proposed by Thomas Merton, or the "object of ultimate concern" in Tillich's understanding of faith.[23]

However, numerous critics think that positing anything common between the religious traditions of humanity as a basis of dialogue is unwarranted and dangerous. Philosophers like Francis Schüssler Fiorenza and Richard Rorty are troubled by what they perceive as "objectivism" and "foundationalism." By these terms they mean the conviction that there must be some permanent ahistorical essence or framework to which we can finally appeal in determining the nature of rationality, knowledge, truth, reality, or religious experience—attitudes both think are highly inappropriate "modernist" attitudes in our current "postmodern" age. Rather than looking for a common ground above or beyond the plurality of religious traditions, Fiorenza and Rorty enjoin us to accept the notion that all knowledge is "theory-laden." Different religious are different "plausibility structures" so that every particular religious tradition is plausible only within its own "language game." There can in principle, Fiorenza and Rorty argue, exist no common reference point upon which to stand to assess the meaning and truth claims made within each of the religious traditions. Different religious traditions are, in other words, "incommensurable."[24]

Christian theologians like John Cobb and Raimundo Panikkar are also highly critical of "objectivism." They warn that the search for any universal should be abandoned. Panikkar's critique is particularly harsh. A genuine religious pluralism, he thinks, cannot and should not imagine a universal system of thought. For him, a pluralist "system" is a contradiction" and the "incommensurability" of ultimate systems is unbridgeable."[25] Likewise, Cobb is critical of John Hick, Wilfred Cantwell Smith, Paul Knitter, and me. He thinks that looking for something common to all religious traditions is to abandon religious pluralism to ahistorical reductionism. It is better, Cobb concludes, simply to be open, which he thinks is inhibited unnecessarily if we state in advance what all religious traditions have in common. The danger is, Cobb rightly points

23. Toynbee, *An Historian's Approach to Religion*, 261–83; Smith, *The Meaning and End of Religion*, chaps. 6–7; and Smith, *Faith and Belief*; Stace, *Mysticism and Philosophy*; Merton, *The Asian Journal*, 309–17; and Tillich, *Dynamics of Faith*, 1–40.

24. See Fiorenza, *Foundational Theology*, 283–311; and Rorty, *Philosophy and the Mirror of Nature*.

25. Panikkar, "The Jordan, the Tiber, and the Ganges," 110.

out, that we might miss what is genuinely different, and therefore what is genuinely challenging, in religious traditions other than our own.[26]

In fact, Cobb regards this danger as so likely that he suggests that there is no one "ultimate" within or beyond the world's religious traditions. Rather, he thinks there might be "multiple ultimates" and that religious pluralists like Huston Smith, Wilfred Cantwell Smith, John Hick, Paul Knitter, and me are afraid to face this possibility.[27] I am forced to admit that proposing that the religious traditions are similar to auxiliary hypotheses that function like a "protective belt" in their particular reference to the "hard core" of my research program does indeed run the risk of imperialistically imposing my theoretical construction on religious traditions other than my own. Furthermore, I am fully aware that many serious Buddhists, Hindus, Muslims, Jews, Christians, Sikhs, and other religious persons will not wish to speak about their experiences mediated through their own particular religious traditions and practice as a common referent to which all religious traditions symbolically point.

Still, even as critics forcefully warn against the pitfalls of objectivism, they just as forcefully warn against radical skepticism based on a debilitating relativism that so locks the religious traditions of humanity within their own particular language games and plausibility structures as to make dialogue between them impossible. Fiorenza, Rorty, Panikkar, and Cobb, paradoxically, assert the possibility of dialogue between the world's "incommensurable" religious traditions. In doing so, they look for a path between objectivism and relativism by asserting that even though there exists no common referent or "ground" among the world's religious traditions, persons inhabiting different religious traditions can still, and should, talk to and understand one another.

How this is possible is not often clear. Cobb and Panikkar simply trust the *praxis* of communication to reveal common experiences, shared problems, and shared viewpoints and plunge into dialogue. They believe that whatever "common ground" emerges in the dialogue can suffice to overcome incommensurability (e.g., between *śūnyatā* and God in Cobb's theology) and lead to mutual understanding and "mutual transformation."[28] Similarly, even as Panikkar disavows universal

---

26. Cobb, "Beyond Pluralism," 81–95.

27. Ibid. Also see Fiorenza, *Foundational Theology*, 202–29.

28. Cobb, "Buddhist Emptiness and the Christian God," 86–90.

theories of religion, he still invokes a single "aspiration" or a single "inspiration" that in some unexplained way unifies all religious traditions.

What Cobb and Panikkar have apprehended is that different religious traditions cannot be ultimately different, as, say, apples are different from granite, in an interdependent, interconnected universe. If they are, how or why or should or could interreligious dialogue even happen? My point is, anyone affirming the value of interreligious dialogue as a "practice" (*praxis*) tacitly affirms that there *does* exist a referent that bonds the religious traditions together, even in their differences, and it serves no purpose to deny it. The problem is how do we indicate this referent explicitly? My proposal for a pluralist research program is a theoretical framework for making the implicit assumption of interreligious dialogue—the existence of a referent to which the religious traditions of humanity point—explicit.

I have in past publications tried to be explicit about what I perceive to be the referent underlying the plurality of humanity's religious faith and practice.[29] In this chapter I refer to this referent as the Sacred. All references to the Sacred—even the term *the Sacred*—are metaphorical in nature. I do not claim that this metaphor is the only one suitable for conceiving the referent to which humanity's religious traditions point. But whatever the metaphor, what it points to is a boundary condition that transcends verbal limitations. So while it is possible, or even likely that using *the Sacred* as the metaphor for naming the referent for humanity's religious traditions might be a mistake, what is not likely is the nonexistence of a referent to which religious traditions of humanity point in their distinctive historically contextualized ways.

THE QUESTION OF EVIDENCE

In the natural sciences, a research program requires evidence supporting its coherence and "fruitfulness," meaning its ability to experimentally predict and confirm conclusions coupled with its capability for accounting for unexpected "anomalous" data that the hard core did not originally predict, but which can be incorporated into the program through changes in the structure of its auxiliary hypotheses in ways coherent with the hard core. The question is, what counts as evidence, and how does evidence relate to experience? In the natural sciences, the

---

29. See Ingram, *Wrestling with the Ox*, chap. 2.

gathering of data subjected to experimental verification supports conclusions. Furthermore, the foci of scientific investigation are the physical
relationships that explain natural phenomena. The explanatory power of
a scientific research program originates in the narrowness of its focus,
which means that most scientific conclusions have little direct bearing
on how human beings actually experience the world.

For example, one of Newton's discoveries was his three laws of
motion, which assume that the natural tendency of a body is to keep
moving forever. But our actual experience of moving bodies on planet
Earth is that they always come to a stop, usually rather quickly, unless
we keep pushing them. According to Newton's laws of motion, the explanation of this paradox is that friction acts to prevent a body from
doing what its natural tendency dictates. According to Murphy, this is
an example of a "broken symmetry," because the conservation of energy
one would expect to see in a freely moving body, described mathematically in Newton's equations, is not what we actually observe in practice.
So the true nature of motion is hidden by the way a body empirically,
that is, actually, moves.[30] In this sense, Newton's laws of motion are as
counterintuitive as the nonlocality of quantum events in contemporary
physics, because they do not easily conform to our everyday experience.

Of course, the evidence supporting the pluralist research program
I am proposing is incapable of experimental repetition. Furthermore,
evidence supporting a nonscientific research program is mostly experiential and historical, socially and culturally contextual, often intensely
private but at the same time communal and not repeatable, and subject
to a number of philosophical, historical, and theological interpretations
over time. This means that a theological research program, as well as the
pluralist research program I am proposing, is concerned with a wider
body of experience than scientific research programs: individual and
communal religious experience, aesthetic experience, ethical experience, philosophical questions, and social justice issues that scientists
intentionally exclude from scientific inquiry. So what does constitute
evidence in support of my particular pluralist research program?

While my own particular experiences cannot be universalized, I
shall begin with reference to how certain aspects of my scholarly work in
history of religions seems to me to constitute evidence pointing to a referent common to humanity's religious experience. Since other scholars

30. Murphy and Ellis, *On the Moral Nature*, 43.

in my field have reported similar experiences, what follows is, I believe, supporting evidence for the fruitfulness of pluralism as a research program. In my case, study of and dialogue with non-Christian traditions and persons have deepened my own understanding of Christian faith and practice.

The experience of the Sacred is pretty much a now-you-see-it-now-you-don't affair, particularly for scholars. Sometimes, an insight flashes through a text or a conversation or a ritual practice, then dissolves into intellectual and emotional fog. But I have read Lord Krishna's instruction to Arjuna in the Bhagavad Gita about the incarnations of Brahman into an infinite pluralism of deities, and this has helped me comprehend the possibilities of God's incarnation in the historical Jesus as the Christ that unifies the pluralism of Christian faith and practice. I have read Buddhist Pure Land texts through Shinran's eyes and have apprehended with him the "other-powered" grace of Amida Buddha's universal compassion, and this has helped me comprehend the grace of God that Augustine, Aquinas, and Luther discovered in St. Paul's Epistles when they thought and wrote about faith. I have read how Elijah hiding in a cave on Mount Horeb met God in "thundering silence" (1 Kings 19:11–12), and that has led me to see how the One God recited by Mohammed in the Qur'an can be closer to a person than a jugular vain; this has clarified for me Christian monotheistic experience of God's interdependent transcendence and immanence.

These experiences, and others emerging from my scholarship, have often stunned me to silence. They constitute examples of partial evidence that the religious traditions of humankind point to, but never fully reveal, a common referent that I have named the Sacred in my work in history of religions, and which I name God when I am engaged in specifically Christian theological reflection. The reality of this referent is more than can be named by any specific religious tradition because whatever this reality is, it conceals itself even as it reveals itself with eye-catching nonchalance. Humanity's religious traditions reveal as much as they conceal, and much depends on questions asked and the assumptions through which the Sacred is experienced and interpreted.

There also exists public evidence in support of my pluralist research program, by which I mean experiences shared in common even though such public experiences are tweaked and interpreted according to the particular traditions that filter these experiences to their participants.

A meaningful way to conceive of this evidence is by means of the "bridge" metaphor suggested by Paul Knitter in his preface to *The Myth of Christian Uniqueness*.[31] One can think of the pluralist research program as a bridge by which one can dialogically cross into the varied traditions constituting the world's religious traditions while avoiding exclusivist theologies of religions (all religious traditions other than my own are false) and inclusivist theologies of religions (to the degree that religious traditions other than my own look like my own, they are vehicles of salvific truth) to pluralist theologies of religions.

Issues of relativism constitute a "historical-cultural bridge." In fact, this particular "bridge" is the starting point for most reflection on the nature of pluralism and is built on an impelling awareness of historical consciousness. Historical consciousness is awareness of the historical-cultural boundary limitations of all knowledge and religious beliefs, coupled with the difficulty of judging the truth claims of another culture or religious tradition on the basis of one's own. This is why Gordon Kaufman claims that a necessary condition for interreligious dialogue is that the participants recognize the historical relativity of all religious beliefs and practices and thereby abandon all claims of theirs being the only or the highest form of religious belief and practice.[32] John Hick notes that if any religious tradition is going to make claims of superiority, it must do so on the basis of "an examination of the facts," that is, some form of empirical data available to all. Hick believes that such data would have to be found in the ability of a particular religious tradition to promote the welfare of humanity better than other religious traditions. He doe not think such data is available. He writes, "it seems impossible to make the global judgment that any religious tradition has contributed more good or less evil, or a more favorable balance of good over evil, than the others . . . As vast complex totalities, the world religious seem to be more or less on a par with each other. None can be singled out as manifestly superior."[33]

It is not only the fact that our religious perceptions are historically relative—I think "relational" is a better word—but also that the object of religious experience is, when all is said and done, a mysterious boundary beyond all forms, exceeding every grasp of it. This is the "mystical

31. Knitter, "Preface," ix–xii.
32. Kaufman, "Religious Diversity," 3–15.
33. Hick, "The Non-Absoluteness of Christianity," 30.

bridge" attested to by all religious traditions, so that the ineffability of the Sacred Mystery demands religious pluralism and forbids any single religious tradition from possessing the only or final truth about the Sacred. Wilfred Cantwell Smith was a champion of this "theological-mystical bridge" until the day he died.[34] He used the notion of "idolatry" to state why pluralism should be the attitude governing interreligious dialogue. "Idolatry" describes not only other religions traditions, but also any attempt to absolutize one's own. Because "Christianity has been our idol," he writes, Christians have too easily given in to the temptation to equate Christianity with God by making Christian faith, like God, absolute and final. Repenting of this idolatry means ceasing all exclusive or inclusive claims and to be open to the "possible equality of other religious traditions with one's own."[35]

Raimundo Panikkar and Stanley Samartha are Christians who draw on Hinduism to lay a mystical foundation for Cantwell Smith's warnings against Christian idolatry.[36] For them, the Sacred is the Ultimate Mystery and is as ineffable (*neti-neti* or "not this-not that" of Upanishadic teaching) as it is a boundary source of cognitive dissonance. All religious traditions reflect as they participate in the Mystery in their own limited and unique ways, but none can own it or claim absolute truth about it. Panikkar is particularly insistent on the limitations of reason. For him, the Sacred is not only ineffable but also radically pluralistic. So too is all reality, as Whitehead suggests. Thus Panikkar concludes that most pluralist thinkers do not really know what radical pluralism means. Pluralism tells us that there is no "one" that can be imposed on "many"; there will always be "one" and "many," which means there will always be differences and disagreements about the "one" Sacred reality named differently in the plurality of the many religious traditions of humanity. Therefore, pluralism does not allow for a universal religious system. The impossibility of a universal religious system is, for Panikkar, a revelation of the nature of the Sacred itself. Accordingly, a pluralist research program should not be understood as a universal system, but a hermeneutics of interreligious dialogue that explores what the religious traditions of the world as auxiliary hypotheses have revealed about the Sacred.

34. Knitter, "Preface," x.

35. Smith, "Idolatry in Comparative Perspective," 53–68.

36. See Samartha, "The Cross and the Rainbow: Christ in a Multireligious Culture," 69–88; Panikkar, "The Jordan, The Tiber, and the Ganges," 89–116.

The need to promote justice points to what Knitter calls the "ethico-religious bridge." Two considerations in this regard require specification. First, the ethical principles and practices of the major world religions seem universal in their focus on compassion, love, honesty, and justice. For example, the practice of compassion that stems from Buddhist experience interpreted through its doctrine of interdependence can easily be affirmed by Christians, Jews, and Muslims even though each tradition nuances these moral values according to their specific worldviews. Second, issues of justice that all human beings face are not religion specific. Gender injustice, racial injustice, social and economic injustice, violence, and environmental injustice are not Christian, Buddhist, or Muslim issues. They affect all human beings regardless of religious affiliation or lack of religious affiliation. The fact that persons of different religious traditions who experience injustice have worked together in what is now called "social engagement" to promote justice constitutes strong evidence for the research program I am proposing. Such socially engaged dialogue does not require that religious persons share common a worldview. Yet the differing worldviews of the major world religions promote social engagement with the forces of injustice running riot in human communities.

For example, Marjorie Suchocki and Rosemary Radford Ruether have clarified how Christian exclusivism has led to "an outrageous and absurd religious chauvinism." They think that holding Christian tradition as the "norm" for judging all other religious traditions is just as exploitive as are sexist assertions of male experience as the universal norm of humanity that creates injustice against women.[37] Knitter goes so far as to say that given the shared moral intuitions of the religions of the world, the starting point and guide for the practice of interreligious dialogue should be something like a "preferential option" for those persons most in need as the primary context for the meeting of the world religions.

Evidence supporting pluralism as a research paradigm is not merely a matter of similarities in doctrines, teachings, experiences engendered by practices, or common ethical principles that cut across the boundaries of specific religious traditions. There are also differences between the religious traditions of the world, differences that express "nonnegotiables" that define the unique character of that tradition. For

---

37. Suchocki, "In Search of Justice," 149–61; and Ruether, "Feminism and Jewish-Christian Dialogue," 137–48.

example, Christian experience and teaching regarding the incarnation is not something Christians can compromise in the practice of Christian faith and still meaningfully participate in a distinctively Christian faith community. Likewise, Islamic monotheism is a call not to reduce God to that which cannot be God and surrender to it, which means no Muslim can accept any form of the Christian doctrine of incarnation and remain within the House of Islam. Buddhist nontheism and Jewish, Christian, and Islamic monotheism are incommensurable. Even as reading the Bhagavad Gita still clarified Christian experience of the incarnation for me, Christian teaching of a single incarnation of God in a particular human life is incommensurable with the Gita's notion of the many incarnations of Brahman in the deities of Hindu experience and teaching. What Buddhist's mean by Awakening is not identical with what Christian tradition means by redemption. The list goes on.

But a pluralist research program need not assume that all religious doctrines and beliefs teach the same things. One need not assume that similar experiences and ideas that cut across religious boundaries possess more evidentiary value supporting pluralism than the "nonnegotiationables" that separate particular religious traditions from one another. In this regard, three points can be made. First, incommensurable teachings, practices, and experiences need not always imply contradiction. Often, differences between religious persons and the communities they represent are complementary. For example, Buddhist practice is thoroughly grounded in nontheism. Yet Christian experience of God as personal also includes experience of God as nonpersonal, as in, for example, Christian mystical theology and practice. Likewise, Buddhist nontheism includes elements of devotional experience and practice in Pure Land Buddhism that seem in many ways experientially similar to Christian theistic experience. While I as a Lutheran think the incarnation points to how God has always worked in the universe, and continues working, the incarnation of God in the historical Jesus does not exhaust the reality of God, which means the faith and practices of non-Christians can teach me lessons I need to understand.

Second, the existence of incommensurable teaching and practices in the world's religious traditions should surprise no one. If my pluralist research program bears correspondence to reality, the religious traditions of humanity are best understood as limited, historically and culturally conditioned means by which human beings have grasped and been grasped by the Sacred. According to most of humanity's religious traditions, the Sacred is boundary beyond the categories of thought and speech. That is, it is an ineffable Mystery that can be glimpsed and experienced contextually in the pluralism of human culture and history, but only partially and incompletely. But just because the Sacred as it is cannot be known completely or expressed in any final way does not mean that human beings cannot say and know something about the Sacred.

Finally, incommensurable teachings may be and often are radically contradictory, as exemplified by Buddhist nontheism and Jewish, Christian, and Islamic monotheism. To Muslims surrendering (*'islām*) to the call of the Qur'an not to reduce God to that which cannot be God, the Christian doctrine of the Trinity can only seem like "idolatry" (*shirk*). Christians who apprehend God incarnated in the life of the historical Jesus as the Christ as the norm of faith must be in disagreement with Muslim teaching that Jesus, while an extraordinary prophet, can never be a redeemer. In such instances, either both doctrines are false or one is true or at least truer than its opposite. But how does one decide given the fact that religious persons faithful to their traditions can only relate to other traditions from the perspective of their own tradition? Human beings seem unable to be religious "in general," but only "in particular"?

In reflecting on this difficult question, it helps to remember that my pluralist research program does not presuppose that all religious doctrines and practices are equally true or that all religions traditions are equally valid. It's very difficult to argue that White Supremacy is a valid form of Christianity or that Islamic extremism and terrorism is an authentic expression of the Qur'an's call that human beings live in peaceful community with one other and with nature. In these examples, distinguishing truth from falsehood is rather easy. But deciding whether Buddhist nontheism or Christian monotheism is a truer account of the Sacred is another matter. While according to this program it is reasonable to argue that the world's religious traditions point to a common referent, it is not reasonable to assert that these traditions are equally true or that one religious tradition is truer than all the rest. No religious person has enough knowledge or experience to make such judgments. We may affirm, for example, that a particular doctrine or practice or religious tradition is the best account of the Sacred *for us*; we cannot do so for someone else. In other words, my pluralist research program requires a confessional approach to theological-philosophical reflection that is expressed through the practice of interreligious dialogue.

In this regard, another point requires clarification. The natural sciences need to be brought into the practice of interreligious dialogue as a contributing partner since in this post-modern age, all religious persons must practice their faith in the context of what the natural sciences are revealing about the physical structures of the universe. What the sciences are revealing both challenge and, if approached with care and sensitivity, deepens religious faith and practice wherever found. According to the Whiteheadian perspective assumed throughout this book, the Sacred, however it is named, is immanent in the very physical processes of the universe. When taken together with the comprehensive explanatory power of the natural sciences, the conclusion must be that the Sacred is "in, with, and under" the universe's unfolding natural processes of which the Sacred is the transcendent reality beyond name and form, holding all name and form together in a unity supporting incredible pluralism. Some of this pluralism constitutes the religious traditions of humanity.

A FINAL OBSERVATION

With the exception of some extremely conservative Christian writers, I can't remember reading any theologian who claims that God is interested in religion. In fact, if one believes the New Testament, God doesn't give a damn about religion, but cares very deeply about human beings and other life forms on this planet. I suspect the same is true in the Tanakh and the Qur'an, although Islam may be the only religious tradition that defines itself as "religion" ('islām). So it seems that the one and only test of a truthful religious idea is pragmatic, or as Jesus is reported to have said, "You know them by their works." A truthful religious idea, doctrine, practice, or religious experience leads directly to practical compassion and love. "Compassion" is knowing by experience the utter interdependence of all living beings, so that the suffering of any living being is one's own suffering, just as the joy of any living being is also, partly, one's own. Compassion engenders love, meaning active social engagement with the world in nonviolent (if possible) struggle against systemic social, economic, and political structures of injustice that cause suffering to human beings and the creatures of nature.

So If one's understanding of God makes one kinder, more empathetic, more impelled to act justly through concrete nonviolent acts of lovingkindness—at least as far possible in a universe in which life must eat life to survive—then one's understanding of God is a truthful construction, even though never fully. I think this is true whether one is a Christian, Jew, Muslim, Hindu or a participant in a nontheistic tradition like Buddhism, or an avowed "secularist." But if one's notion of God has made one unkind, brittle of spirit, belligerent, cruel, or self-righteous, or has led one to kill in God's name, one has an untruthful understanding of God. I also think this is true whether one is a Christian, Jew, Muslim, Hindu, or a participant in a nontheistic religious tradition like Buddhism.

3

A Christian's Dialogue with the Buddha

A NY THEOLOGIAN WHO TAKES religious pluralism seriously knows from experience the cognitive dissonance forced on traditional Christian doctrinal claims by boundary questions, particularly the claim that participation in Christian faith is the sole vehicle for humanity's *salvation*—whatever this might mean. Some years ago, John Cobb wrote an essay the title of which posed the question, "Can a Christian Be a Buddhist, Too?"[1] Cobb's answer was affirmative, but he also thought that Christians making this claim must carefully explain their reasons for making it. Surely, this claim pushes Christian tradition to unexplored boundaries.

I agree with Cobb, but in a dialogue with Buddhism or the natural sciences, it is extremely important that neither be reconstructed through the imposition of the categories of Christian theological reflection so that Christians can affirm the truths of Buddhism or the sciences. Doing so merely creates another Christian monologue posing as dialogue, which to my mind is exemplified by Karl Rahner's notion of "anonymous Christianity" and Hans Küng's distinction between Catholic tradition as the "ordinary" way of salvation" and Protestant and non-Christian traditions as "extraordinary" ways of salvation.[2] This chapter is about why I agree with Cobb's claim that "a Christian can be a Buddhist, too"—even though my specific theological understanding of religious pluralism is

1. Cobb, "Can a Christian Be a Buddhist, Too?" 1–20.

2. I have critiqued Rahner's and Küng's theologies of religions in my book, *The Modern Buddhist-Christian Dialogue*, 47–51. For the specific details of Rahner's and Küng's theologies of religions, see Rahner, *Theological Investigations*, 5:131ff. and related essays in vols. 6, 9, 12, and 14. For Küng's reflection on non-Christian religious traditions, see Küng, *On Being a Christian*, 89–116; Küng, *Christianity and the World Religions*.

somewhat different from his. But first, two preliminary observations are in order.

First, I must confess that much Christian reflection on Jesus and the Buddha, and much Buddhist reflection of the Buddha and Jesus, seems incoherent. I often experience immense cognitive dissonance because I am not always certain what Buddhists and Christians are talking about when they talk about the Buddha and Jesus. It is absolutely necessary that we are clear about the terms employed in theological reflection about the Buddha or Jesus. Which Buddha are Buddhists and Christians talking about? Which Jesus?

So for the sake of clarity, I shall use the term *historical Jesus* to mean "Jesus as reconstituted by historical scholarship," particularly by the Jesus Seminar and other historians, Christian and non-Christian, trying to reconstruct the historical Jesus from canonical and noncanonical texts like the *Gospel of Thomas*. The historical Jesus was a Galilean Jewish peasant born in or near the village of Nazareth between 4 and 6 BCE, who around the age of thirty or thirty-one was baptized by John the Baptist. After his baptism Jesus spent approximately a year traveling in Galilee as an itinerant teacher or rabbi, leading a small band of disciples that included more than the twelve male disciples mentioned in the Synoptic Gospels. Some, perhaps most, of these disciples were women.

He spent the last few weeks of his life in Jerusalem preaching in and around the temple before Passover. As he had in Galilee, Jesus found avid listeners, which angered both the temple priests and many of the leaders of local synagogues, because the Romans could construe his popularity as rebellion against their occupation of Galilee and Judea. He was arrested by the temple leaders, charged with blasphemy, and handed over to the Roman military governor of Judea, Pontius Pilate, who executed Jesus by crucifixion around the year 30.

Jesus was baptized by John the Baptist, but Jesus went far beyond John's apocalyptic preaching about the imminent reign of God. That is, when Jesus found his own voice it was squarely within the Hebraic prophetic tradition's call for social and economic justice, which he connected with his own particular vision of the reign of God, or in more contemporary English translation, the commonwealth of God. Unlike John the Baptist, Jesus taught that the commonwealth of God was immediately present in the struggle for justice on behalf of the poor and marginalized. For him, love and justice were two sides of the same coin.

God, whom Jesus addressed as *Abba* or "Father," is experienced in loving relationships that engender justice. In particular, Jesus thought God's preferential option was decidedly for the poor. Finally, Jesus did not refer to himself as Messiah.[3]

I shall reserve the term *Jesus as the Christ* to mean "the Christ of faith" as portrayed in the four canonical gospels, the epistles of St. Paul and the writings in the rest of the New Testament, in the church's creeds and doctrine, and in Christian experience. The Christ of faith is a theological interpretation of the historical Jesus. The historical Jesus and the Christ of faith are, of course, interdependent, but they are not identical. Both are historical constructions.

Likewise, I shall use the term the *historical Buddha* to refer to Siddhartha Gautama as reconstructed by historical scholarship that focuses mostly on the Pali Canon. Briefly stated, Siddhartha Gautama was born twenty years either side of 550 BCE, probably near the present town of Bodh-gaya in northern India; his Hindu caste was Kshatriya ("warrior"), although he later renounced the institution of caste. Since his father was a local raja, he lived in relative wealth, which in his late twenties he found unsatisfactory. He married and had a son, but he abandoned both his marriage and his son, and entered what Hindu tradition calls the "forest hermit" stage of life to engage in a six-year quest for satisfying answers to troubling boundary questions engendered by his encounter with "old age, disease, and death." Toward the end of this period, he tried ascetic practice, which almost killed him, after which he then engaged in a protracted period of meditation and experienced a breakthrough of consciousness. He then began an approximately forty-year-long career as an itinerant teacher, and gathered together a community of disciples. He died of food poisoning at the age of eighty or eighty-one from a meal gathered by begging from supportive laypeople.

Gautama also taught something like the Four Noble Truths, the doctrine of nonself, and the doctrine of impermanence as descriptions of his own religious experience on the night of his Awakening. His stress on meditation meant that his primary intention was the instruction of monks living apart from engagement with the world as laypersons; the laity major religious role was to support the monastic community and to live a life of merit acquisition by means of following the "five

---

3. See Crossan, *The Historical Jesus*; Hanson and Oakman, *Palestine in the Time of Jesus*.

precepts" (nonviolence, not stealing, not lying, not misusing sex, not drinking intoxicants). Gautama's movement evolved into the first monastic movement in the world's religions.

I shall use the term *the Buddha of faith and practice* (in the sense of what the Noble Eightfold Path calls "right viewpoint" and "right aspiration") to refer to doctrinal descriptions of the Buddha portrayed in the teachings and practices of the various schools and traditions of Buddhism, Buddhist meditative and devotional experience, and the schools of Buddhist philosophy. The Buddha of faith and practice is an interpretation of the historical Buddha encountered in the "buddhaologies" of the various schools of Buddhist cumulative tradition. Therefore the historical Buddha and the Buddha of faith and practice are interdependent, but they are not identical, and both are historical constructions.

Forty-four years of teaching university courses in history of religions and thirty years of dialogical engagement with the Buddhists have convinced me that John Hick's "pluralistic hypothesis" provides an accurate account of the realities of religious pluralism.[4] But as I noted in the in the previous chapter, my assent to the pluralist hypothesis is *not* an assertion that all religious traditions draw identical conclusions about this sacred reality, or that the incommensurable differences between religious traditions are less important than their similarities, or that all religious traditions are equally true or valid. But I do think (1) that all of humanity's religious traditions are historically and culturally contextualized responses to a sacred reality named differently by each tradition; (2) that no particular religious tradition can be said to be superior to another so as to be the sole vehicle of "salvation," defined differently, of course, by each religious tradition; and (3) that since the religious traditions of humanity embody partial glimpses of truth, but never the whole truth about the Sacred, the proper mode of relationship between the world's religious traditions is dialogue, not evangelical monologue.

Or to restate these assumptions in Christian theological language, the sacred reality I name God as incarnated in the life, death, and resurrection of the historical Jesus as the Christ of faith is not contained or constrained by Christian teaching, experience, or practice. God is always more than we can imagine through the categories of Christian theological reflection, which is not to say that we cannot know something important about God through the practice of Christian

4. Hick, *An Interpretation of Religion*, 235–36.

theological reflection. Accordingly, I want to know how other religious human beings have encountered and related to the Sacred they name differently than I so that the knowledge and relationship that I have with God may be deepened and less parochial. In other words, the purpose interreligious dialogue is mutual creative transformation.[5]

While I can't prove it, I think it very unlikely that God has not been without witnesses. Nor is it likely that 3,500 years of Jewish and Hindu tradition, 2,500 years of Buddhist tradition, 2,000 years of Christian tradition, or 1,400 years of Islamic tradition are collective illusions. Human beings are often collectively delusional, but I find it difficult to believe that collective illusions can exist for the great lengths of time that the world's religious faiths have been grasping human beings. Which is not to say that there have not been deluded Jews, Hindus, Buddhists, Christians, or Muslims. But human beings have experienced *something* throughout these millennia mediated by their religious traditions. As a Christian, I want to understand what this "something" is, as a means of creatively transforming my Lutheran participation in Christian faith and practice. Accordingly, the theological assumption that guides what follows is that the reality Christians experience through the incarnation of Christ in the historical Jesus is not exhausted by this incarnation. Dialogue with the religious faith and practice of non-Christian persons—illustrated in this chapter by Buddhism—opens possibilities for deeper understanding and appreciation of Christian faith as well as the faith of our non-Christian brothers and sisters.

ENCOUNTERING THE BUDDHA

I was introduced to the historical Gautama the Buddha and the Buddha of faith and practice for the first time in 1960 in an undergraduate history-of-religions course at Chapman University. That same fall semester I was also enrolled in an Introduction to the New Testament course, where I first encountered the historical Jesus and the Christ of faith. The regard I have for the historical Jesus and the historical Gautama the Buddha was first awakened in those days and has grown stronger over the years. The historical Gautama the Buddha continues to engage me in three ways.

5. Ingram, "Interfaith Dialogue," 77–94; Streng, "Selfhood without Selfishness," 177–94.

First, the Buddha was sophisticated teacher of great insight. His teaching about the Four Noble Truths—that all existence is implicated in suffering and impermanence (*duhkha*); that we cause suffering for ourselves and for others by clinging (*tanha*) to permanence in an impermanent universe; that release from suffering is possible; that the Noble Eightfold Path is the "practice" that leads to the cessation of suffering and the achievement of "awakening" (*nirvāna*)—ring true to my experiences.[6]

But I also continue to think that human beings suffer for systemic reasons having little, if anything, to do with clinging to permanence. For example, processes of natural selection entail suffering that has little to with clinging to permanence. Economic systems like free-market capitalism bring great wealth to a minority of individuals and nations at the cost of institutionalized poverty and environmental degradation for millions of people who are oppressed by the wealthy few controlling the market. The suffering of the poor has little to do with clinging to permanence. Racist institutions cause millions of persons of color excruciating suffering that has little to do with clinging to permanence. The suffering experienced by women oppressed by patriarchal social and political systems has little to do with clinging to permanence. Even so, the Buddha's analysis of the human condition remains a "pedagogical reality therapy," meaning that he accurately described important aspects of the human condition to which faithful Christians should pay attention.

Second, the Buddha's teaching about nonself has helped me understand biblical images of human selfhood. I am certainly not the only Christian to receive this assistance. The doctrine of nonself is interdependent with the doctrine of impermanence. All existing things and events are, according to the Buddha, constituted by nonself (*anātman*), meaning all things and events arise from the ceaselessly changing interrelationships that things and events undergo from moment to moment of their existence. But there is no permanent self-entity or unchanging "soul" that undergoes these changing interdependent relationships. There exist only interdependent relationships undergoing ceaseless change and becoming. Or in more specifically Buddhist language, the

---

6. The particular items included in the Noble Eightfold Path are right viewpoint, right aspiration, right speech, right conduct, right livelihood, right effort, right concentration, and right mindfulness.

process of *pratītya-samuptāda*, meaning interdependent co-arising constitutes all things and events at every moment of space-time.

The doctrine of nonself underlies every aspect of Buddhist tradition. Applied to human beings, "nonself" means that we are not embodi-
ments of an unchanging self-entity or soul that remains self-identical
through time. Buddhist teaching is firm in its rejection of notions of
permanent selfhood and all doctrines of the soul. What "we" are, the
Buddha taught, is a system of interdependent relationships—bodily,
psychological, sociological, cultural, and spiritual—that, in interdependence with everything else undergoing change and becoming in the universe, continuously creates "who" we are from moment to moment in
our lifetimes. We are not permanent souls that "have" the relationships
we experience and undergo; we *are* the interdependent relationships we
experience as we experience them. We don't "have" our bodies and their
functions; we *are* our bodies and their functions. We don't "have" hopes,
fears, joys, sorrows, culture, family, friendships, wisdom, or ignorance;
we *are* the hopes, fears, joys, sorrows, culture, family, friendships, wisdom, and ignorance we undergo and experience them. Because these
relationships are always changing, the "we" that they constitute is always
changing. Consequently, the Buddha taught, permanent selfhood is an
illusion the clinging to which is the source of suffering.

As I indicated a few paragraphs ago, it was my encounter with the
Buddha's teaching about nonself that opened my eyes to biblical understandings of human selfhood.[7] Stated in perhaps too summary a fashion,
contemporary biblical scholarship has conclusively demonstrated that
there is no self-body dualism in biblical portrayals of human selfhood.
For example, St. Paul portrayed the human self as a unity of "soul,"
"body," "flesh," and "spirit" mutually constituting the whole person
through the moments his or her lifetime. None of these elements can
be separated from the total structure of a person's reality. Since, again
according to St. Paul, God created human beings entire, in humanity's entirety human beings must be "redeemed."[8] The soul is not immortal in biblical teaching. When a person dies, all the interdependent

7. See Ingram, *The Modern Buddhist-Christian Dialogue*, chap. 7, for a more detailed comparison between Buddhist and biblical paradigms of human selfhood.

8. My interpretation of the Bible's selfhood paradigm is based on the following
sources: von Rad, *Old Testament Theology*; Bornkamm, *Paul*; Bultmann, *Theology of the
New Testament*, vol. 2; and Ridderbos, *Paul: An Outline of His Theology*.

relations that constitute that person disappear. As Paul Tillich is reported as having said, "When you die, you die." Resurrection is God's restoration of the whole person to a new embodied system of interdependent relationships, but in continuity with previous interrelationships before death. Faithful Christians, St. Paul wrote in 1 Corinthians 15, participate in the resurrection of the historical Jesus the Christ. Resurrection is not identical with the Greek notion of the immortality of the soul through which the classical Christian theology has traditionally, but inaccurately, read the biblical images of human selfhood.

Finally, the Buddha's emphasis on meditation and detachment are two aspects of his practice that have opened me to the possibilities of Christian contemplative traditions.[9] As a Lutheran Christian, and so a member of a faith community in which Christian contemplative practices have often been interpreted negatively as "works righteousness," I have found the Buddha's emphasis on meditation a truly liberating experience. Meditative detachment engenders "presence," and I am not the only Christian for whom Buddhist meditative traditions have been helpful in this regard.[10] Like others, I have incorporated Buddhist meditative practice, in my case the Zen practice of *zazen* or "seated meditation" with Christian traditions of contemplative prayer in my "interior dialogue" with Buddhist tradition and my own Christian faith.

What I have learned most from the practice of *zazen* and contemplative prayer is that as long as you are conscious of yourself, you can never concentrate on anything. Buddhist meditation and Christian contemplative prayer are exercises in the art of self-forgetfulness that allows us to be fully present to others and the interdependent processes of existence itself. As Shinryu Suzuki once put it, "What we call 'I' is just a swinging door which moves when we inhale and when we exhale . . . [W]hen we become truly ourselves, we just become a swinging door, and we are purely independent of, and at the same time, dependent upon everything."[11] Thomas Merton expresses a similar idea from a Christian perspective: "Zen is the very awareness of the dynamism of life living itself in us—aware of itself in us, as being the one life that lives in us all."[12] Sitting in *zazen* and in the Christian discipline of centering prayer has

---

9. Ingram, "On the Practice of Faith," 43–50.

10. See, for example, Johnston, *Christian Zen.*

11. Suzuki, *Zen Mind, Beginner's Mind*, 29.

12. Merton, *Mystics & Zen Masters*, 21–22.

brought me to something like this awareness and has been an important corrective to the disconnected clutter of my conventional experiences.

WHY ARE THESE PEOPLE CHRISTIANS?

In her Buddhist response to Christians writing about the influence of the Buddha on their faith and practice, Grace G. Burford once asked, "If the Buddha is So Great, Why Are These People Christians?"[13] As a Lutheran Christian who reveres the Buddha, I think this is legitimate question. May particular answer to Burford's question is that it is possible for "a Christian to be a Buddhist, too." Accordingly, the remainder of this chapter will focus on Burford's question: given my reverence for the Buddha, why am I a Christian and a Buddhist too, who happens to participate in the Lutheran community of faith and practice?

My dialogue with the historical Gautama the Buddha and the Buddha of faith and practice is what John Dunne described as a process of "passing over and returning,"[14] a process that has led me in many instances to go "beyond dialogue."[15] By this I mean that my dialogue with the Buddha has taken me beyond the conventional boundaries of Christian faith and practice into Buddhist experience, wherein I have learned and appropriated truths I think I have perceived. This movement has been followed by a return to the "home" of my Lutheran brand of Christian faith and practice—enriched, renewed, and I hope creatively transformed.

The dialectic of passing over and returning has been part of my theological reflection for fifty years, and, I think, it describes the experiences of most Christians and Buddhists engaged in dialogue with the world's religions. And while many Christians and Buddhists have not returned to the home of their own traditions after undertaking the adventure of dialogue, and while some Buddhists and Christians now

---

13. Muck and Gross, *Buddhists Talk about Jesus*, 131–37.

14. Dunne, *The Way of All the Earth*, chap. 1.

15. Cobb, *Beyond Dialogue*, chap. 3. In Cobb's view, passing "beyond dialogue" does not mean that the practice of dialogue need stop. Ideally, the practice of theological reflection is a dialogical process, both with the world's religions and with the natural sciences. The phrase "beyond dialogue" is his way of naming what Dunne refers to as "returning." For Cobb, going beyond dialogue implies continually being *in* dialogue as part of the process of one's continual growth in Christian faith. He assumes the same process occurs for Buddhists too who, faithful to Buddhist tradition, go "beyond dialogue" with Christian tradition.

identify themselves as "Christian-Buddhists" or "Buddhist-Christians" because of dialogue, I find myself increasingly convinced of the truth of Christian faith and practice even as I am convinced of the truth of Buddhist faith and practice.

I do not mean that I find everything in Christian tradition of value, and especially not the theological imperialism of Christian fundamentalism and much evangelical neo-orthodoxy. Nor do I think everything that wears a Buddhist label is in harmony with the Buddha's teachings. Dialogue does not mean being uncritical about the truth claims of any religious tradition, including one's own. Some elements of Buddhist teaching and some elements of Christian doctrine are incommensurable: for example Buddhist nontheism and Christian theism, or the Buddha's strong emphasis on self-effort as necessary for the achievement of awakening and the Pauline, Augustinian, Lutheran, Calvinist doctrine of justification by grace through faith alone. In the practice of dialogue, one must be "as wise as serpents."

So, for example, while I think theism offers the most coherent interpretation of how the universe works in light of what contemporary scientific cosmology and evolutionary biology have revealed, I also have Buddhist friends who think current scientific cosmology supports Buddhism's nontheistic worldview. For this reason alone, inviting the natural sciences to participate as a "third partner" in current Buddhist-Christian dialogue should add new dimensions to the mutual creative transformation that Christians and Buddhists experience through dialogical encounter, and might even lead to the creative transformation of the natural sciences themselves.

Sociological factors also come into play in the formation of one's religious identity. Chances are, had I been born in Saudi Arabia or Kuwait, I would be a Muslim. Had I been born in Sri Lanka or Thailand, chances are I would be a Buddhist. Had I been born in Ireland, Spain, or Italy, chances are I would be a Roman Catholic. Of course, while cultural factors do not *determine* one's religious identity, and while persons can and do choose to move from one inherited religious tradition to another, or choose to leave a religious tradition altogether, sociological, cultural, and historical factors play a transformative role in the experiences of faithful people in all traditions.[16] My particular Christian identity is

---

16. See Berger, *The Heretical Imperative*, for an important analysis of religious faith in the contemporary world from the perspective of sociology of knowledge.

contextualized by the accident of my birth in the postmodern, technologically sophisticated, religiously plural, consumerist culture of the United States.

As I argued in chapter 1, while it may not be quite correct to claim that "truth is relative," the religious claims to which persons commit themselves are constructed and "relational" in the sense that we can only experience and know anything from the historical, cultural, and gender contexts we occupy at the moment we claim to know anything. An important conclusion I draw from these assumptions is that I cannot claim that my conclusion that a Christian can be a Buddhist too is normative for anyone other than me. Nor do I mean that Christian tradition is superior to Buddhist tradition. I can only reasonably speak from my own experiences and hope it helps others with their theological reflection.

So why am I a Christian, given my veneration of the Buddha? The Buddha's teaching about meditative detachment as a means of living fully in the present without illusory pretenses seems true to my experiences. Many of these realities are painful, which means that waking up to the interdependent structures of existence as they are engenders compassionate interaction with all living beings, which in turn is the foundation for what the Vietnamese Zen Buddhist monk, Thich Nhat Hanh, calls "social engagement."[17] The Buddha's path to liberation—acting without desire for personal success with goodwill toward all living beings—creates a form of non-ego-centered consciousness that can deal with life's rough-and-tumble without pretenses. Such consciousness can produce marvelous social outcomes. Similar experiences are engendered by the practice of Franciscan, Jesuit, and Benedictine contemplative disciplines. It was my interior dialogue with Zen meditative practice that gave me access to the contemplative traditions of Christianity, the practice of which engenders experiences and social results quite similar to Buddhist tradition.

But I have never achieved the radical self-sufficiency upon which the Buddha insisted. "Be lamps unto yourself," he taught. According to the *Dīgha-nikāya*, which contains some of the earliest texts in the Buddhist Canon, his last instruction to his disciples was, "You should live as islands unto yourselves, being your own refuge, seeking no other refuge; with the Dhamma as an island, with the Dhamma as your refuge, seeking no other refuge . . . Those monks in my time or afterwards live

17. Nhat Hahn, *Being Peace*.

thus, seeking an island of refuge in themselves and in the Dhamma and nowhere else, these zealous monks are my monks and will overcome the darkness (of rebirth)."[18]

In other words, the structure of Buddhist experience and the structure of Christian experience are different. While Christians can, and sometimes do, experience the Buddha as the Awakened One, Buddhists seem unable to experience Jesus as the Christ because of the specifics of the Buddha's path and the way this path fleshes out in the experience of practicing Buddhists. Buddhist tradition seems much more worldview specific in this regard than Christian tradition.

I do not mean that Buddhist tradition is inferior to Christian tradition. Nor am I implying that either Buddhism or Christianity is an expression of religious imperialism, which is not to say that there have not existed imperialist Buddhists or Christians. My intention is descriptive; I am suggesting that a difference exists between the structure of Buddhist experience and the structure of Christian experience. Given that I am a Christian, the structure of my experience is more like St. Paul's: "I do not understand my own actions. "For I do not do what I want but I do everything that I hate," and "I do not do the good I want but the evil I do not want is what I do" (Rom 7:15, 19). Bonnie Thurston's description of St. Paul's experience also reflects my own: "In the struggle to be a lamp unto myself, I am brought face to face with Jesus Christ. There are many points of comparison between the Buddha and the Christ, and many helpful comparisons have been drawn. I want to focus on one that I have not seen: the attitude of each toward his followers. The Buddha says, "Be lamps unto yourselves" and "one is one's own refuge." The Christ says, "Come to me, all you that are weary and are carrying heavy burdens, and I will give you rest" (Matt 11:28)."[19]

I know from experience my own inability to be a lamp unto myself. Of course, lack of self-discipline and personal ignorance play a part in my experiences, as anyone who knows me can attest. But something else always seems to block my path toward the self-fulfillment the Buddha described as Awakening. The Christian word describing this "something" is *sin*. Sin is not simply immoral action. Sin is individual and collective egoism that is ontologically ingredient within the structure of human existence that separates us from God and other human beings.

18. Cited in Schumann, *The Historical Buddha*, 246.
19. Thurston, "The Buddha Offered me a Raft," 124.

That is, sin is constituted by the illusion of permanent selfhood, according to which individuals and communities act as if they are the center of the universe. Or in more Whiteheadian language, sin is placing one's own subjective aim for oneself over God's initial aim that we achieve the maximum intensity of harmonious interrelationship with all occasions of experience, harmony—meaning a whole that is greater than the sum or its parts.

Accordingly, sin is, to my way of thinking, an individual and communal expression of what Buddhists call *taṇha*, the egoism inherent in trying to prove to ourselves that we are permanent selves, from which we cannot free ourselves. Sin is thereby the source of human suffering and the suffering of other life forms on this planet. All one has to do to confirm that sin is ontologically ingredient in human existence is to read a daily newspaper or watch the local and international news on television. So given my personal experiential confirmation of the reality of sin, my experiences have taught me that taking refuge in myself is an illusion because there is no permanent self in which to take refuge. I need to take refuge in, that is, trust, a reality operating externally to my self and yet part of my self, a reality Christian tradition names *grace*.

The source of grace is God's love, which Christians apprehend incarnated in the historical Jesus as the Christ of faith. Trusting God's grace and not one's own self-reliance is *faith*. It is through grace that God interacts with us and everything else in the universe at every moment of space-time since the creation of space-time. The primary source of my understanding of God's graceful character is, of course, what I have learned from the history of Christian theological reflection and experience. But I have also learned much about grace from Jewish and Islamic tradition, as well the thirteenth-century writings of Shinran, the founder of the True Pureland School (*Jōdo Shinshū*).[20]

Of course, all this is perhaps too "confessional" for a Christian scholar of history of religions. Furthermore, my experience should not be uncritically universalized. I think what Buddhists experience as Awakening has happened, and still happens, to the Buddha's disciples. But I also think what the Buddha meant by *awakening* and what Christian tradition means by *redemption* are not identical, which need not imply that Awakening and redemption are contradictory experiences or concepts. In fact, I tend to understand the Buddha's teaching

20. See Ingram, *The Dharma of Faith.*

regarding Awakening and Christian teaching of redemption as complementary concepts that point to similar experiences—in the sense of the notion from the Epistle of James that "faith without works is dead."

What I mean is that the historical Gautama the Buddha helps me focus on the realities of existence. So does the historical Jesus, especially in his teaching that God's love favors the poor and the oppressed. In this sense, I am a Christian and a Buddhist too. But it is in Jesus as the Christ that I think I apprehend the source of grace that I think flows over this universe like a waterfall, which does not mean that non-Christians do not experience grace through their distinctive traditions and practices. But however apprehended, grace is a gift from God offered to all human beings regardless of the religious labels they wear—as well as to everything that lives—that frees us from having to worry about ourselves, our awakening, our redemption, our "success," so that we can focus on the practice of "loving/compassionate wisdom" without regard to achieving something we think we lack, as if we were on the outside of our lives looking in.[21]

Wisdom, in both the Buddha's teaching and in Christian mystical theology, is the experience of the utter interdependence of all things and events at every moment of space-time. The Buddha's teachings were focused on disciplines meant to engender the experience of interdependence and nonself for his disciples. Interdependence is also asserted in the Christian doctrines of creation and incarnation as this is understood through the lenses of the Prologue to the Gospel of John and confirmed in the experience of Christian faith. The experience of universal interdependence is the source of compassion—where compassion is experiencing the suffering of all sentient beings as one's own because they are; and where love means socially engaged action in the world's rough-and-tumble struggle for peace and justice.

A LUTHERAN'S INTERIOR DIALOGUE WITH BUDDHISM

Until 2006 I earned my living practicing the craft of history of religions. In Lutheran theological language, this is my "calling" and "vocation." I know this to be true because of how I was first opened to an amazing world of religious pluralism fifty years ago during my first undergradu-

---

21. See Ingram, *Wrestling with the Ox*, 126–31, for a fuller explanation of what I mean by "loving/compassionate wisdom" as the practice of faith.

ate history-of-religions course at Chapman University. I am still amazed by this world. The history of religions continues to ground my theological reflection and energizes both my exterior conceptual dialogue with Buddhist doctrine and my interior dialogue with Buddhist meditative practice.

So until my retirement from Pacific Lutheran University in 2006, my vocation was teaching an academic field of inquiry I love to young people as I engaged in research and writing. I was paid for doing this by a university related to the Evangelical Lutheran Church in America that bills itself as a "new American university" located in one of the most culturally pluralistic and beautiful regions in the United States. While I'm not sure what a "New American University" is, I am certain I had a great gig. I am equally sure that my professional life constituted for me evidence of the grace that Christian tradition in general—and Luther's theology in particular—describes as flowing "in, with, and under" this universe at all times and in all places.

Of course, all this is highly confessional. Yet when it comes down to it, all theological reflection is confessional. We can only write about our own particular interior journey as this is informed by the particular community of faith that gives context to our faith and practice, for it is not possible that persons can be "religious in general," but only in particular.[22] Yet sometimes, a few historians of religions and some Christians and Buddhists are able to participate in communities of faith and practice other than their own. This too seems to me a visible sign of an invisible grace.

I have learned an important lesson from interior dialogue with Buddhists as this shakes out in my particular practice: it strikes me as a bit glib to suggest that the focus of practice is *God* or, if Buddhist, *Emptiness*, because I often feel intellectually blindsided by what people who practice mean by these words. The question is always epistemological: what *do* these terms mean as we practice whatever we practice? Plenty of theological-philosophical propositions can be strung together to answer this question, and, I think, it is impossible not to guide practice by theological-philosophical reflection. But we must never cling to belief in propositions, for the moment we do, they hide the reality to which they point. Conceptualizing and believing in rational

---

22. This is a modified restatement of an observation by George Santayana. See Santayana, *Interpretations of Poetry and Religion*, chap. 9.

propositions is a necessary beginning because it is a form of "faith seeking understanding." But faith is never, in Christian or Buddhist tradition, identical with belief in propositions. Faith happens when we are grasped by and bet our lives on (that is, when we trust) the reality to which propositions may sometimes point—and the grasp of this reality is a grasp that goes beyond propositions, is not caused by propositions, yet cannot be experienced nonpropositionally, since even the statement, "God or "Emptiness is beyond the grasp of language" is still a proposition.

Much also depends on the meaning of *practice*. The clearest discussion of the meaning of *practice* I have found is a remarkable essay written twenty-five years ago by John C. Maraldo, titled "The Hermeneutics of Practice in Dogen and Francis of Assisi."[23] Maraldo notes that the popular understanding of practice is instrumental: practice (*praxis*) is something different from theory (*theoria*); theory and theoretical knowledge are ends in themselves; practice is an end outside itself.[24] Much discussion of practice within the context of Buddhist-Christian dialogue assumes this popular understanding. For example, one often hears from Zen Buddhists and advocates of Christian "spirituality" that doctrines are meaningless, that the mind should be emptied of such theoretical stuff so that what's *really* real about reality can be experienced directly by a mind unfettered by theoretical constructions. Seen from this perspective, practice is an instrumental means of achieving something we don't think we have. So one practices meditation or contemplative prayer in order to achieve a "beyond-all-language" experience of awakening or union with God.

Such instrumental understandings that bifurcate practice from achievement presuppose that we need to do something to achieve whatever it is we don't think we have, as if we were on the outside of our lives looking in. But this does not quite square with Christian contemplative traditions and Buddhist meditative traditions, and it is certainly contrary to Luther's teaching about faith and grace and his rejection of all "works" as instrumental means of creating a redemptive relationship with God.

Buddhist tradition, Roman Catholic and Orthodox contemplative tradition, and mainline Protestant tradition agree on this point: we have everything we are ever going to have, and there is nothing to gain—absolutely nothing—through practice, because practice and attainment are

23. See Maraldo, "The Hermeneutics of Practice," 53–74.
24. Ibid., 54–55.

nondual. For me as a Lutheran Christian, therefore, religious practice is the disciplined performance of faith without regard for achieving goals, if you will, a kind of Christian "actionless action" (Chinese: *wu-wei*), since faith is not something I decide to "have" by any act of the will to believe. One *finds* oneself in a state of faith, one does not *practice* oneself into a state faith, since there is no time when we or any other thing or event in the universe is ever separated from God—at least according to the Genesis creation story as read through the Prologue of the Gospel of John.

Of course, this presupposes St. Paul's, Augustine's, and Luther's teachings that grace operates universally at all times and in all places in this universe. For me, this means that if one is engaged in a religious practice, one is drawn to it by grace through faith alone, which means there is nothing to gain by practice that one does not already have. Within Buddhist tradition, Shinran's teaching that even Awakening itself is created in us by Amida Buddha's compassionate "other-power" points to a parallel Buddhist understanding of the experience of the utter interdependence of grace, faith, and practice.[25]

Any activity that takes practice will do to as an illustration. Practice activities like learning a musical instrument or dance, learning a language, practicing a martial art, doing floral arrangement or the tea ceremony, or writing poetry require repeated effort and concentrated performance. Such activities are daily disciplines exercised for no other reason than their performance—unless one is a novice who mistakenly interprets practice as different from skilled performance. But as an activity becomes "practiced" and proficient performance is acquired, the gap between what we will and what we do gradually disappears. "It may even be said that during any practice there is no room for desires or intentions which separate our present performance from an imagined ideal, what we are doing from how we wish we were doing it."[26] Consequently, my particular "practice" has evolved into three interdependent expressions: (1) theological reflection, (2) centering prayer, and (3) social engagement.

According Patricia O'Connell Killen, theological reflection is a discipline that becomes an art by its practice. She defines *theological*

25. I have made note of these parallels in several past publications. See Ingram, *The Dharma of Faith*, chap. 4; and Ingram, "Shinran Shōnin and Martin Luther," 447–80.

26. Maraldo, "The Hermeneutics of Practice," 54.

reflection as "the discipline of exploring individual and corporate experience in conversation with the wisdom of a religious heritage. The conversation is a genuine dialogue that seeks to hear from our own beliefs, actions, and perspectives, as well as those of the tradition. It respects the integrity of both. Theological reflection therefore may confirm, challenge, clarify, and expand how we understand our own experience and how we understand the religious tradition. The outcome is new truth and meaning for living."[27]

While the above quotation was written from a Roman Catholic perspective, what it says about theological reflection can be extended to other religious traditions because the structure of the art of theological reflection is a dialogical process with five interdependent movements: (1) reading a text one enters into his or her experience and (2) encounters feelings or emotional responses engendered by the text; (3) paying attention to these feelings generates images; (4) attending and questioning images may lead to insight; (5) insight leads, if we are willing, to action, part of the meaning of which for me is "social engagement."[28]

The art of theological reflection is not identical with academic theology, although my commitment to academic theological discourse continues to contextualize my particular practice of theological reflection. Nor is the art of theological reflection identical with what Catholic monastic theology calls *lectio divina* ("divine reading"), although there are similarities. Specifically, I tend to focus on Christian and non-Christian texts as well as remembered conversations and experiences that seem to me transformative. Part of my practice is to read the New Testament through once a year, usually in the summer when I have more quiet time, guided by a single question.[29] My reasons are both scholarly and personal: I think historians of religions must first understand and appreciate their own religious tradition before they are in a position to adequately understand and appreciate religious traditions other than their own even as practice needs to be grounded in the foundational traditions of one's community.

27. Killen, *The Art of Theological Reflection*, viii.

28. Ibid., chap. 2.

29. Evangelical theologian and participant in Buddhist-Christian dialogue Terry Muck introduced me to this practice over dinner in 1999. My question then was related to the death of my father in April of that year: "What does the Jesus saying, 'To live your life you must first lose it,' mean?"

I also include the Psalms and other texts from the Tanakh as objects of theological reflection, as well as Buddhist texts like Santideva's *Bodhicaryavatara* ("Entering the Path of Awakening"), the writings of Martin Luther and Martin Luther King Jr.; the poetry of William Butler Yeats and T. S. Eliot; the writings of Thich Nhat Hanh and Annie Dillard; the journals of Thomas Merton, and, most recently, the mystical theology of thirteenth-century women mystics like Marguerite Porete. The writings of John Cobb, Wilfred Cantwell Smith, Huston Smith, Ruben Habito, and John Hick; the novels of John Steinbeck and my friend Jack Cady; the Buddhist reflections of Sallie King and Rita Gross; and the theology of religions of Paul Knitter—so deeply energized by his passion for social engagement—are also examples of texts I have appropriated for theological reflection.

For me the process involves keeping a journal because I am convinced that writing is a mode of meditation and that we never adequately understand a thing until we write it down. I do not engage in this practice expecting specific experiences or insights. Instead, I try to allow the process to take me where it takes me, like going on a journey without a destination or map. So as I read a text during this practice I begin by reflecting on the experience the text occasions and try to accurately describe its inner and outer dimensions—what the particular experience is to me in relation to its objective content—in order to be fully aware of the source and nature of the experience. In other words, the intent is to attend to the experience's positive, negative, or neutral "emotional tone," in Japanese, its *mono no aware* or "feeling of things," by nonjudgmentally describing it, simply noting what the feelings are, in order to live consciously "inside" the experience because this is the best position from which to reflect.

By entering an experience and narrating it nonjudgmentally, one discovers that it is drenched with feeling. This is so—probably in disagreement with standard Buddhist teaching—because our capacity to feel, to respond with our entire being to reality, is the essence of our nature as enfleshed persons. That is, feelings are embodied affective and intelligent responses to reality as we encounter it, so that feelings join mind and body and are the most human responses to reality, to "the way things really are," that we possess. It is through feelings that we encounter reality incarnated in our lives.[30]

30. Killen, *The Art of Theological Reflection*, chap. 2.

It is important to carefully observe feelings and emotional states because they embody a holistic response to our existence and are a source of insight. The process is full of promise, but often full of danger. The danger comes in two ways: (1) being overwhelmed and mired in feelings so that we subjectively grovel in them, or (2) being deadened to them. Both responses block insight. So the stage of attending to feelings involves being aware of them, without denying them or clinging to them, so that they can be identified clearly and accurately.

The next step entails giving shape and voice to feelings in the language of symbolic imagery. People do this in normal conversation all the time, as, for example, when my grandfather would say of a person he thought was ignorant, "He wouldn't know sheep shit from raisins if it was in the same pie," or when a sad person says "I feel like a motherless child," or when someone describes her friend as "having a heart of gold." Images work differently than conceptual language. Images are more total, more closely tied to feelings, and less rationalized. Images create ways for feelings to be included in our world of meaning, thereby expanding our world by more immediate inclusion of new experience.

Sometimes musing on an image pushes us to new insights and frees us to respond to reality in ways never before imagined. This is because images can compress many aspects of a situation into an integrated, intense, wholeness, while at the same time opening us to new angles of vision. In the process, images help us break free from habitual ways of interpreting our lives by propelling us to discover new meanings. At other times, pondering an image leads to unexpected surprises. Images capture the core of a situation by shifting from the original descriptive narrative to a symbolic structure. In this way, they engender insights and open doors to new ways of apprehension and self-awareness. Powerful insights can also empower action in the form of social engagement, consideration of which will be given after a brief description of centering prayer.[31]

Centering prayer is a method of refining one's intuitive faculties so that one can more easily enter contemplative prayer, which Thomas Keating describes as developing one's relationship with God to the point of communing beyond words, thoughts, feelings, and the multiplication of acts; "a process of moving from the simplified activity of waiting upon God to the ever-increasing predominance of the Gifts of the Spirit as the

---

31. Ibid.

source of one's prayer."[32] For Thomas Merton, centering prayer was a way of "entering the Silence."

Although I suspect that God is found everywhere, including the noise of our lives, human beings experience God most clearly in silence—Jesus in the silence of the desert for forty days, the Buddha sitting in meditation for forty-nine days (although he didn't name what he found in the Silence *God*). I am certainly not an accomplished mystic like Keating, Merton, the Buddha, or Margarete Porete. But like Merton, I have come to think that the silence is all there really is. It is the alpha and Omega. It is God brooding over the face of the deep, the blended notes of ten thousand things, the wine of wings, the music of Bach and Mozart, the physics of Einstein and Bohr. "We take a step in the right direction to pray to this silence," wrote Annie Dillard. "Here all distinctions blur, and we quit our tents and pray without ceasing."[33]

Centering prayer has much in common with certain aspects of Buddhist meditation, especially *zazen*, since unlike theological reflection, centering prayer is a discipline designed to withdraw attention away from the ordinary flow of conscious thoughts and feelings through which we tend to identify our selves. It aims to expand awareness of a deeper dimension of selfhood not completely sayable in words, yet to which words can symbolically point. Mahayana Buddhists call this dimension of selfhood the true Self.

According to Christian mystical theology, the true Self is the image of God in which every human being—in my opinion, all things—are created. So centering prayer, as I understand it, is a method of deepening the experience of interdependence, which in Christian teaching is affirmed theologically by the doctrines of creation and incarnation. Traditional Catholic theology understands centering prayer as preparatory to "contemplation," that process whereby the *image* of God incarnated in us as our true Self is transformed by grace into a *likeness* of God, so that we might apprehend the created universe as God apprehends it and love all things accordingly.

The technical details of my particular practice of centering prayer are fairly simple. For two thirty-minute periods a day—morning and evening—I take a comfortable sitting position in a quiet place while avoiding positions that cut off circulation so that bodily discomfort will

32. Keating, *Open Mind, Open Heart*, 146.

33. Dillard, *Encounters with Chinese Writers*, 76.

not block concentration. I begin by taking a few deep breaths, and, while breathing slowly and evenly, shut my eyes and begin withdrawing my senses from ordinary activity. With closed eyes, I bring to conscious attention what Thomas Keating calls a "sacred word" that expresses my intention of opening and surrendering to God. I don't repeat this word aloud, but rather use it as an interior object of concentration.

The purpose here is not to suppress conscious thoughts and feelings because that is not possible. The intention is to "observe" thoughts and feelings as they pass in review without stopping them or holding on to them. Whenever I catch myself holding on to a thought or feeling, I gently bring the sacred word into conscious focus until the thought or idea moves on. In this way, as the stream of conscious thoughts and feelings is gradually quieted, one becomes centered and open to whatever there is beyond the limitations of thoughts and our emotional responses to them.

In summary, centering prayer is essentially an exercise in letting go, a method of allowing, without forcing, our ordinary train of thoughts and feelings to flow out. It is a kind of waiting without expectation designed to bring the interdependence of the present fully and consciously into focal awareness. According to Keating, practicing centering prayer with expectations or goals takes us out of the present and projects us into an imagined future that is most probably a reflection of our present ego trips. So centering prayer is a method of waking up to the presence of God in, with, and under the present interdependent moment without attachment to or anxiety about the future. As I noted above, Thomas Merton described this practice as "Entering the Silence"[34]—a process that does not require being a monk or a nun and, from both a Christian and Buddhist perspective, always energizes social engagement.

One of the important lessons I have learned from students and colleagues practiced in social engagement is that interreligious dialogue is not merely an abstract conversation between religious persons on this or that doctrine. Interreligious dialogue—as well as the practices of theological reflection and centering prayer—requires involvement in the rough-and-tumble of historical, political, and economic existence. Or to paraphrase the Epistle of James, "theological reflection, centering prayer, and interreligious dialogue without works is dead" for the same reasons that "faith without works is dead." For me, a central point of the

---

34. Merton, *Entering the Silence*, 2,

practice of faith is the liberation of human beings and all creatures in nature from forces of oppression and injustice and the mutual creative transformation of persons in community with nature. Both the wisdom that Buddhists affirm is engendered by Awakening and the Christian centering prayer point to the utter interdependency of all things and events—a notion also affirmed by contemporary physics and biology in distinctively scientific terms.[35]

Awareness of interdependency engenders social engagement because awareness of interdependence and social engagement are themselves interdependent. Thus we experience the suffering of others as our suffering, the oppression of others as our oppression, the oppression of nature as our oppression, and the liberation of others as our liberation— and thereby we become empowered for social engagement, which Thich Nhat Hanh described as "Interbeing."[36]

Consequently, socially engaged dialogue needs to focus on practical issues that are not religion specific or culture specific, meaning issues that confront all human beings regardless of what religious or secular label persons wear. My running thesis about practice is in agreement with Christians like Martin Luther, Martin Luther King Jr., and Mother Theresa; the Vietnamese Buddhist monk Thich Nhat Hanh and the Thai Buddhist layman Sulak Siveraksa; the Hindu sage and activist Mahatma Gandhi; as well as Jewish call that we struggle for justice in obedience to Torah, or the Islamic call to surrender to Allah guided by the Qur'an: that religious faith and practice do not separate us from the world. The practice of faith throws us *into* the world's rough-and-tumble struggle for peace and justice. Any practice that refuses to wrestle with the world's injustices is as impotent as it is self-serving. Accordingly, whatever practice we follow needs to be guided by a concern for the liberation of all sentient beings, for as both Christian and Buddhist teaching affirm, we are all in this together. Distinctively Christian practices and, I suspect, distinctively Buddhist practices cannot have it any other way.

35. See Peacocke, *Theology For a Scientific Age*, 39–43, for a wonderful summary of the current consensus among scientists regarding the interdependent and interconnected structure of the physical universe.

36. Thich Nhat Hanh, *Interbeing*.

4

Is This All There Is?

NOTHING IS MORE CURIOUS than the self-satisfied dogmatism with which humankind at every point in its history cherishes the delusion of the finality of its existing modes of knowledge. In this sense, skeptics and believers are alike. At this moment in history, scientific materialism and Christian fundamentalism are the leading dogmatisms.

Standing against both is Charles H. Townes, a 1964 Nobel Prize laureate in physics and a 2005 Templeton Prize laureate. He has been confronting scientific and theological boundaries all of his professional life. Among his accomplishments was the discovery of the principles of the laser in 1951. After an intensely frustrating day in his lab running headlong into experimental dead ends, he left his laboratory and headed to a park bench in Washington, DC. When he sat down to relax and clear his mind, it suddenly came to him, a "revelation as real as any revelation described in scriptures." He then applied his "revelation" directly to the invention of the laser, for which he awarded his Nobel Prize.[1]

Townes describes the relation between science and religion as a convergence emerging from the similarities they share in spite of differences. This convergence happens when both meet at the boundary limits of each discipline. Both science and religion seek to explain (1) how the universe works, and (2) how the meaning of the universe works. While science and religion do not draw identical conclusions about how the universe works or how meaning in the universe works, the parallels between them are as striking as the differences. As science seeks to understand *what* the physical universe is like and *how* the universe works, including human beings, so religion aims at understanding the *meaning* and *possible purpose* of the universe, including the meaning

---

1. Townes, "Marriage of Two Minds," 36–43.

79

of human existence. For Townes, science and religion are best understood as complementary human ways of understanding the universe's structure of existence because if it true that the universe is purposeful and meaningful, whatever meaning might exist must be reflected in the physical structures of the universe that engage scientists. Science and religion are not rivals.

William Stager makes a similar point in his essay, "The Mind-Brain Problem."[2] He notes that the "laws of nature" encompass two interdependent meanings: the physical regularities, processes, and structures in nature (1) as we know and understand them, and (2) as they actually function in reality. Natural laws reveal the underlying unity of nature because they testify to nature as a universally embedded rationality evidenced by the power of mathematics to describe these processes. Which means, as Einstein said, the greatest mystery of the universe is that we, through reason, can comprehend it. Which does not mean that we can comprehend everything about the universe. It's the *how* questions that reveal the universe's exquisite rationality.

This is so, Stager argues, because in the realm of the very small (i.e., subatomic particles) to the very large (the cosmos as such), the extraordinary applicability of mathematics in describing the structures, entities, and physical processes of nature enforces the conclusion that there is indeed an underlying unity to all things and events in the universe at every moment of space-time since the first nanosecond of the big bang until the universe's eventual cold death trillions of years from now. But the *how* questions upon which science focuses bleed into the *why* questions of other disciplines, especially of theology and philosophy. It is at the intersection of these *how* and *why* questions that the rationality embedded in the universe, coupled with and the mystery that human beings seem to be able to understand the physical processes of nature, that make belief in God *reasonable*. Yet even so, the universe's rationality and the mystery of why it should exist in the first place—along with we who ask such questions—do not constitute *proof* of God's existence.

This chapter will follow Townes's and Stager's lead and argue that dialogical engagement between science and religion should tell us something important about each, as well as something about the structures of the universe. Furthermore, understanding either science or religion requires the use of logic, evidence (rational analysis of experience in

2. Stager, "The Mind-Brain Problem," 130.

religion, experimentation in the sciences), carefully chosen assumptions, intuition, and faith. It is at the point of faith that the convergence between science and religion starts.

It is abundantly clear that faith is as operationally important for scientists as it is for religious persons. Of course, much depends on the meaning of the world *faith*. In contemporary English usage, *faith* is the assertion of an opinion without sufficient evidence to call one's opinion *knowledge*. For example, one often hears the assertion that Christian doctrines like the incarnation or the resurrection must be accepted "on faith," apart from rational argument for or against these doctrines. But this is a misunderstanding of the meaning of *faith* in all the world's religions.[3] Faith is never the irrational act of believing something to be true or false in spite of evidence, as in the notion that something must be "accepted on faith."

Whether in a religious or a scientific context, faith is an act of "trust," a way of "betting one's life" that involves the whole person, that is, the intellect, the emotions, and the body, and is thereby the foundation for knowing anything at all, as in St. Anselm's formulation, "faith seeking understanding." Beliefs may be elegant, informed, uninformed, stupid, superstitious, true, or false. Beliefs may even express faith. But beliefs, as such, can neither be faith nor engender faith. So, whether a scientist, a Christian historian of religions engaged in theological reflection, or a Buddhist engaged in *zazen,* betting one's life on an opinion is a highly irrational act and never conducive to attaining knowledge. It is also an act of "unfaith." However, once finding oneself in a state of faith, one is empowered to draw reasonable conclusions and beliefs that sometimes contribute to real knowledge.

While it is not widely understood that the natural sciences involve assumptions based on faith, scientists in fact "trust" that a rational order underlies the structure of the physical processes at play in the universe that they can't "prove" to be the case by the application of scientific methods. Without such faith, science cannot proceed. In fact, nothing in the natural sciences is absolutely proven. It was the mathematician Kurt Gödel who demonstrated that to prove anything, there must be an overall set of assumptions one can trust, even though one might never prove that these assumptions are even self-consistent. Scientists must make the best assumptions based on reasoning about physical experi-

---

3. See Smith, *Belief and History*; Streng, *Understanding Religious Life.*

ence they can, and must have faith, that is, trust, that this will lead to reliable knowledge about the physical structures of the universe.

More specifically, scientists trust that there is an underlying unity in the universe that is testified to by nature's universal rationality that scientists continue to verify successfully in their work. In the realm of the very small (the subatomic) and the very large (the cosmos), the extraordinary applicability of mathematics continues to reinforce this trust, which is scientific faith seeking understanding.

Therefore, scientific methods can be reduced to two principles: (1) all theory, ideas, perceptions, instincts, and prejudices about how things are must be tested against external reality—what they are—through direct experience of the universe itself; (2) this testing must be publicly repeatable. One-time private experiences are not acceptable as scientific theory or conclusion. What *is* accepted from private sources (like "thought experiments") are suggestions about what *might* be true pending experimental verification—here creativity comes to play in science. The "discovery of facts" depends on prior expectation, meaning how scientists " look" at the universe engenders the "facts" they "discover" in the universe. "How scientists look" can mean anything from which apparatus is used in a laboratory to how the natural sciences allocate funds over the next decade.

Falsification also plays a central role in scientific theory because scientists expect a theory to make predictions for future testing. It is not enough simply to specify what to look for to show that the theory is correct. A theory should also specify what to look for that would show the theory is incorrect. Finally, no scientist, no matter how dedicated to the scientific method, insists on believing only what has been winnowed out as "truth" by scientific methods. Indeed, some scientists spout this rhetoric, but no scientist actually lives by it. All scientists accept plenty of evidence coming by means having nothing to do with scientific methods.

The role of faith in scientific methods is also empirically evident since there are as many mysteries in science as there are in religion. For example, physicists know only 5 percent of the matter and energy composing the universe. What is the nature of the remaining 95 percent, now vaguely referred to as "dark matter" and "dark energy," matter and energy being two interdependent sides of the same physical reality, according to Albert Einstein's theory of special relativity? It is clearly detectable in the universe's expansion, but at this date, *what* dark matter or energy is remains a mystery.

Here is another example: Scientists also assume that the laws of physics have been the same everywhere in the universe from that point of time after the big bang called Planck time until the present. Planck time is 10^{-43} seconds after the big bang, when the size of the universe was at Plank length, or more precisely the time it takes light to travel to Planck length. Planck length is 10^{-37} centimeters, the size of the universe at Planck time. Prior to Planck time, the laws of physics seem to have been absent, or at least not detectable, which is why cosmologists have not been able to determine the exact nature of the event at t=0.

Given the convergence between science and religion that Charles Townes describes, a Buddhist-Christian trialogue with the natural sciences and theological reflection influenced by this trialogue should be beneficial. This is so because the physical processes of the universe set boundary constraints not only for what scientists can know but also what theologians can know. The most expedient means to support this thesis is to focus on the scientific origin story of the universe and current scientific speculation about the universe's probable end. It must be understood that this cosmological narrative is undergoing continual modification as new evidence is discovered. Not all cosmologists are in agreement with the "standard big bang" model, so what I shall describe is the current "majority report." Furthermore, while being a challenge to all traditional religious beliefs and practices, big bang cosmology also provides a common narrative story that is capable of inclusion in the wisdom of all religious traditions in their own distinctive ways.

THE COSMOLOGICAL NARRATIVE

Some 13.7 billion years ago the contents of the universe were together in an initial singularity, meaning a region of infinite curvature and energy density at which the known laws of physics are not known (t=0).[4] There was a "big bang." The history of the cosmos began approximately three minutes after this event, when protons and neutrons were combining to form nuclei. Five hundred thousand years later, atoms were coming into existence. One billion years from t=0, galaxies and stars began forming, followed by planets at ten billion years. After another two billion years, microscopic forms of life began to form appear on our planet.

4. See Halliwell, "Quantum Cosmology," 477–97.

A universe with life is different from a universe without life, and the big bang origin narrative must include the origin of life, both on this planet and most probably elsewhere in the universe. The fact of evolution has been established with the kind of certainty attributed to such physical facts as the roundness of the earth, the heliocentric motions of the planets around our Sun, and the molecular structure of matter. Evolution is descent with modification over time. All contemporary living organisms on the earth share common descent with modification from microbial life of the simplest type—called prokaryotes, which are cells whose nuclear material is not bounded by a nuclear membrane— which existed about three billion years ago. Natural selection drives evolution, which is a process of change and diversification in life forms over time that seems rooted in the genetic structure of all living organisms. Apparently, evolution does not reverse itself but is unidirectional toward the future, much like what cosmologists call the "arrow of time," which can never, as far as anyone knows, reverse itself.[5]

This cosmological narrative demonstrates physically what Buddhists and Christians have apprehended philosophically and theologically: all things and events that have ever have existed, now exist, or will exist are interrelated and interdependent from the very beginning. We are relatives of the stars, the oceans, the earth, and all creatures that have lived, now live, or will live. The entire universe is physically interdependent and organic in structure, a dynamic reality, constantly moving and becoming, always in process. This implies that the universe is open ended, ever creative of novelty, things and events never before imagined, yet always coming to be in interdependence with what went on before; again, these notions should bring a smile of recognition to all Buddhists and Christians, particularly process theologians.

But there is more too. In 1988, two groups of astrophysicists, one led by Brian Schmidt and the other by Saul Perlmutter, using similar techniques, were looking for a specific kind of explosion called a type-1a supernova, which occurs when an aging star collapses in on itself in a gigantic thermonuclear explosion. Type-1a supernovas are so bright that their light can be seen all the way across the universe and is uniform enough to have its distance from Earth calculated with great accuracy. This is important, because as Edward Hubbell discovered, the whole

---

5. For a fuller description of this cosmological narrative, Ingram, *Buddhist-Christian Dialogue in an Age of Science*, 4–9.

universe is expanding in all directions at any time, with more distant galaxies receding from Earth faster than nearby galaxies. So Schmidt's and Perlmutter's teams measured the distance to these supernovas (deduced by their brightness) and their speed of recession from the earth deduced by the reddening of their light, known as the Doppler shift.

After analyzing this information, both teams discovered that something very odd was going on. In the 1980s, astrophysicists believed the universe's expansion would eventually slow down, either gradually or rapidly, depending on the amount of matter contained in the universe— an effect that was expected to show up as distant supernovas appearing brighter than one would expect when compared to closer supernovas. But the more distant supernovas appeared dimmer, which meant that the universe's expansion was speeding up, which suggested that the universe's expansion was speeding up, which in turn suggested that some sort of "dark energy," now called antigravity, is forcing galaxies to fly apart against the gravity pulling them together. This means that there is more antigravity pushing the galaxies apart at an accelerating rate than there is gravity pulling the galaxies together—which means that the universe will expand forever unless forces now unknown to cosmologists are at work.

Most cosmologists think that the universe will infinitely expand, so that a rather bleak picture of the universe's final end is emerging in the scientific community. The hundred billion galaxies that can be observed through the Hubble telescope and telescopes on earth will zip out of range. Tens of billions of years from now, the Milky Way will be the only galaxy detectable from Earth, although it is not likely that anything will be alive on our planet by that time. Other nearby galaxies, including the large Magellanic Cloud and the Andromeda Galaxy, will have drifted into and merged with the Milky Way. Our sun will shrink to a white dwarf and enter into a long lingering death that could last for a hundred trillion years, about a thousand times longer that the universe has existed to the present date. The same will happen to most other stars, although a few will end as blazing supernovas. All that will be left will be black holes, the burnt-out residues of stars, and whatever remains of dead planets. Finally, by the time the universe is one trillion trillion, trillion, trillion, trillion years old, these black holes will disintegrate into stray particles, which will bind loosely enough to form individual "atoms" the size of today's universe. Eventually, even these will decay, leaving a featureless,

infinitely large void. And that will be that. For many scientific reduction-
ists, the "fundamentalists" who generalize scientific conclusions through
the filter of materialist metaphysics, this is "all there is."

Still, most astronomers and physicists are typically more cautious
than most theologians and philosophers and insist that the discoveries
about dark matter and dark energy, as well as the apparent flatness of
space-time must be confirmed before they can be finally accepted. There
will probably be more surprises to come: the idea of a cosmological
constant—a notion that Einstein rejected as his biggest mistake—is now
the leading candidate for understanding dark energy. However, dark
energy could be a force that reverses directions at some point in space-
time to reinforce, rather than oppose, gravity. But if the current view
holds up, that the universe's expansion continues, then some of the most
important questions in cosmology—the universe's age, what it's made
of, and how it will end—will be answered only seventy years after these
questions were first posed. And well before the end of cosmic history—
further in the future than human minds can grasp—humanity, perhaps
even biology, will have vanished. Yet it is conceivable that consciousness
of some sort might survive, perhaps in the form of a disembodied digital
intelligence.[6] If true, this intelligence will notice that the universe has
become a vast, cold, dark, lonely void.

If this is really all there is, the universe seems pointless and empty
of value, and the conclusions that Steven Weinberg draws from big bang
cosmology, Richard Dawkins's interpretation of evolutionary history,
and E. O. Wilson's theories of social biology and genetic determinism
appear to accurately describe the way things really are, as opposed to the
way religious persons might like things to be. If the universe is indeed
pointless and without meaning, Christian, Jewish, and Islamic doctrines
and practices are collective illusions having no basis in physical fact.
Theravada and Mahayana Buddhist doctrines and practices, Hindu
tradition, Confucian tradition, Daoist tradition, along with the primal
traditions of Native Americans and other tribal cultures, are likewise
illusory. This means that all Christian theologies of religions are meaningless, which means that the practice of interreligious dialogue and
dialogue with the natural sciences is reflection on ideas that correspond
to nothing that can actually exist.

6. See Tippler, "The Omega Point as *Eschaton*," 217–53.

And yet, as physicist-theologian John Polkinghorne reminds us, scientific inquiry is narrowly focused and limited—bits of the physical processes of nature that can be analyzed through repeatable experimental procedures described mathematically.[7] The brilliant intellectual power of the natural sciences in revealing the universe's physical structures and the technological application of this knowledge comes at the price of ignoring most of what human beings experience. For example, while the methodological reductionisms of physics can easily explain why we hear sound because of the vibration of air molecules striking our eardrums, physics cannot explain my or anyone else's love of classical music, jazz, bluegrass, or folk music or of the poetry of William Butler Yeats or T. S. Eliot; or why other people prefer other styles of music and poetry. While biology can explain the evolutionary history of the human eye, it cannot explain why a fall light show on Puget Sound—when after a passing rain shower, the setting sun paints the water and trees in acrylic orange—always stuns me to silence. Seen from the wider parameters of human experience, the materialist reductionisms of Weinberg, Wilson, and Dawkins seem more like incoherent metaphysics than scientific description.

This is so because reductionist "bottom-up" scientific descriptions of physical reality do not describe, "all there is." As John Hick never tires of pointing out, all religious human beings share a common "religious intention" not to delude themselves about the way things really are in the universe,[8] which is not to say that religious persons do not often delude themselves. Religious faith and practice can be, and often is, an opiate, as Karl Marx wrote, an anesthesia that deadens one's intellect and emotions, a prophylactic to shield oneself against contamination from the disagreeable realities of existence or from other religious traditions. But Marx was also partly wrong, and profoundly so. Historically, the most creative human advances have been in what the Chinese called *wen*; that is to say, in "the arts" that civilize human beings. In the arts, culture in its widest meaning, human beings are placed in contact with reality and with what is distinctive about being human. The arts of all cultures, including the natural sciences, are grounded in the religious traditions of those cultures.

---

7. Polkinghorne, *Belief in God in an Age of Science*, chap. 2.

8. Hick, *An Interpretation of Religion*, chap. 11.

Nevertheless, the natural sciences, particularly scientific cosmology, evolutionary biology, and the collection of scientific disciplines known as the cognitive sciences, pose serious challenges to all religious traditions. If it is confirmed that the universe's expansion will continue forever, the universe seems condemned to futility, and human existence is a transient episode in the cosmos's transient history, and theological reflection has butted head-on into a boundary that seems impenetrable. A bleak prognosis indeed that calls into question the evolutionary optimism of such writers as Pierre Teilhard de Chardin, who believed that the evolutionary processes of the universe are leading to the universe's final fulfillment in at "Omega point."[9]

For Christian theological reflection—and Jewish and Islamic reflection—the issue is divine action. Scientists now describe the physical processes at play in the universe, from its beginning at Planck time to its probable ending trillions of years from now without reference to God's interaction with any physical process past, present, or future. If one assumes, as theologians must, that God created the laws of nature that "govern" the universe from its beginning until its end, the question is how God can be active in natural events without suspending or breaking the natural laws God created, which scientists discover. Retreating to deism will not do, since deistic theologies offer no solutions to such questions as the problem of incredible suffering in an evolutionary universe; that is, how a just and loving God can allow such suffering to be part of God's creation—in which God is no longer involved. For theological reflection engaged in dialogue with the natural sciences, the issue is one of finding a "causal joint" that allows God to be active in the universe without violating the laws of nature through which God created (*creatio ex nhilo*) and continues creating (*creatio ex continua*) the universe.

COSMOLOGICAL CHALLENGES TO CHRISTIAN THEOLOGICAL REFLECTION

In *Buddhist-Christian Dialogue in an Age of Science*,[10] I noted that physicist-theologian John Polkinghorne agues as a physicist that "scientific theories and models and beautiful equations should prove to be the clue to understanding nature; why fundamental physics should be possible;

9. Teilhard de Chardin, *The Phenomenon of Man*.

10. Ingram, *Buddhist-Christian Dialogue in an Age of Science*, 41.

why our minds have such ready access to the deep structure of he universe. It is a contingent fact that this is true of us and our world, but it
does not seem sufficient simply to regard I as a happy accident. Surely it
is a significant insight into the nature of reality."

However, as a Christian theologian he concludes:

> I believe that Dirac and Einstein, making their great discoveries,
> were participating in an encounter with the divine . . . There is
> much more to the mind of God than physics will ever disclose,
> but this usage is not misleading, for I believe that the rational
> beauty of the cosmos reflects the Mind that brings it into being
> . . . I do not present this conclusion as a logical demonstration—
> we are in the realm of metaphysical discourse where such cer-
> tainty is not available believer or unbeliever—but I do present it
> as a coherent and intellectually satisfying understanding.[11]

For Polkinghorne, the boundary constraints of physics lie in the
fact that physics is incompetent when confronted with ethical, aesthetic,
and religious experiences that are the concern of theological reflection.
To which I would add, also in agreement with Polkinghorne, that the
ethical, aesthetic, and religious experiences that concern theological
reflection in separation from what science tells us about the physical
processes of the universe cannot provide assistance in understanding physical processes *or* moral, aesthetic, and religious experience.
Theology *must* be in dialogical engagement with the natural sciences;
the natural sciences *should* be in dialogue with Christian theology as
well as world's religions.

If standard big bang cosmology is an accurate portrayal of the
physical origins of the universe, it seems reasonable to ask what caused
the big bang—a boundary question cosmologists cannot scientifically
answer. The standard Christian (and Jewish and Islamic) answer is that
God created the universe. But there is a problem with the Christian doctrine of creation that at first glance seems to point in the direction of
Buddhist nontheism. The problem is that cosmologists claim that the
big bang marked not only the beginning of the universe but also the
beginning of time. Time did not exist before the big bang, so there could
have been no cause of the big bang. "What place then for a creator?" asks

---

11. Polkinghorne, *Belief in God in an Age of Science*, xiii.

Stephen Hawking in *A Brief History of Time*, to which one might add, "or divine agency in the continuing processes of nature?"[12]

The Buddhist answer to Hawking's question is that there is neither room nor need for a creator, which means the challenge big bang cosmology poses to the Christian doctrine of creation is crystal clear. One way some theologians have responded is by reflecting on the relation between space and time in the scientific origin narrative. As I understand this narrative, the big bang was an unusual explosion because it did not take place at a particular location in space because there is no space outside the big bang. A common analogy scientists use to imagine this conclusion is a rubber balloon to which a number of coins are glued. The coins represent galaxies. As air is pumped into the balloon, it expands. Suppose a fly were to land on one of the coins. What would it see? All the other coins moving away from it, which is, of course, the observed motion of galaxies relative to cosmologists studying them from Earth.

Most astronomers now think that the motion of the galaxies is due to the space between galaxies expanding, rather than to the galaxies moving through space; because, as Einstein's general theory of relativity has it, space and time are welded together into a four-dimensional continuum called "space-time." Space does not exist without time; time does not exist without space. In Buddhist language, they are "co-originated." So every galaxy in the universe is being carried outward from the big bang singularity on a tide of expanding space-time, just as coins glued to a balloon are carried apart by the rubber surface as the balloon expands. Furthermore, just as there is no empty stretch of rubber surface "outside" the surface where the coins are glued, so there is no empty three-dimensional space outside where galaxies are found. It is this interpretation of the recession of the galaxies that leads cosmologists to conclude that all space and time that now exist were squashed to an infinitesimal singularity at the big bang. In other words, space began as nothing and has continued to expand ever since.

In agreement with Stephen Hawking, Buddhists believe that this particular aspect of scientific cosmology gets rid of the sort of creator god most people have in mind when the think of the two creation stories in Genesis 1 and 2: an eternal deity who first exists alone and then

12. Hawking, *A Brief History of Time*, 141. Hawking makes similar observation about the "place" for God in his revision of this book, titled *A Briefer History of Time*, 137–42.

decides, for reasons known only to God, to create the universe. God says some words; there is a big bang and, wham!, creation begins. Indeed if the word *God* refers to this sort of entity, Buddhist nontheism seems more closely allied with current scientific cosmology than Christian monotheism. However, much depends on the meaning of the world *God*. Consider the following quotation from St. Augustine, written in the fourth century: "It is idle to look for time before creation, as if time can be found before time. If there were no motion of either a spiritual or a corporal creature by which the future, moving through the present, would succeed the past, there would be no time at all. We should therefore say that time began with creation, rather than creation began with time."[13]

In other words, for God there exists neither before nor after. God simply *is* in a motionless eternity. Time and space are part of creation. Before creation there exists neither time nor space, and therefore "nothing." Deeply influences by Platonic philosophy, Augustine wrote as early as his *Confessions*, "It is not in time that you [God] precede all times; all your 'years' subsist in simultaneity, because they do not change; your 'years' are 'one day' and your 'today' is eternity."[14]

Time exists because things change, Augustine argued. In Buddhist language, all things and events change because all things and events are interdependently impermanent. If nothing changed (if nothing "moved," in Augustine's language), we could not distinguish one point of time from another, and there would be no way of knowing to what the word *time* referred. Therefore, Augustine argued, if there were no objects that change, that is, "move," there would be no objects at all. Which means, *time* would be a meaningless category. Furthermore, if there is no time, there is no space ("ether") through objects move or that they occupy. In other words no moving objects, no time; no time, no space.

Most contemporary Christian theologians continue to follow Augustine's lead by distinguishing between ontological and historical origination. Like Augustine, most conclude that space and time are as much a property of the universe as anything else, and it makes no sense to think of God's predating the creation of the universe. This means that there is an important distinction between the words *creation* and *origin*.

13. Augustine, *De civitate dei* (*The City of God*), XII,15), quoted in Stannard, "Where in the World Is God?" 4.

14. Augustine, *Confessiones*, book 11; *Confessions* 230.

While in everyday conversations, we might use these words interchange-ably, in Christian theological discourse since Augustine, each word has its own distinctive meaning. For example, if one has in mind a question about how the universe began, one is asking a question about historical origins. Origin questions are empirical matters for scientists to decide; their current research points to the standard big bang cosmology.

But the notion of creation is an ontological concept that poses is-sues different from the question of the universe's historical origins. In Christian teaching, creation has as much to do with the present instant of time as any other instant. Why is there something and not nothing? Why are we here? To whom or what do we owe our existence? What keeps us in existence for a finite length of time? In a universe of such creativity and beauty, why is there so much suffering? In universe of such universal suffering, why is there so much creativity and beauty? Christian theological reflection on creation concerns the underlying "ground" of all things and events in space-tine, past, present, and future.

Process theologian and physicist Ian Barbour continues Augustine's argument in his interpretation of the doctrine of creation *ex nihilo* in light of standard big bang cosmology. In his *Religion and Science*, he makes as sharp a distinction between ontological/historical categories as Langdon Gilkey makes in *Maker of Heaven and Earth* (which is a neo-orthodox restatement of Augustine's distinctions).[15] According to Barbour, creation is an ontological issue and is the central meaning of *ex nihilo*, or "out of nothing," while $t=0$ in big bang theory is an empirical issue and plays no role in the doctrine of creation *ex nihilo*. So, Barbour advises, it is unwise for theologians to employ big bang cosmology as a means of demonstrating the reasonableness of Christian theism.

However, in his analysis of Barbour's views, physicist-theologian Robert John Russell argues that *should* an initial singularity ($t=0$) be supported scientifically (which entails getting evidence before Planck time about the physical processes at or nearer the singularity), Barbour would conclude that such evidence *would* provide an "impressive ex-ample of dependence on God."[16] It is still the case, however, that Barbour continues to sharply distinguish between ontological origin and histori-

---

15. See Barbour, *Religion and Science* 128ff.; Gilkey, *Maker of Heaven and Earth*, 310–15.

16. Russell, "Finite Creation," 302.

cal beginning and places the weight of his theology of creation on the ontological interpretation of the universe's creation.

The point I wish to make is that Buddhist and scientific materialist criticism of the Christian doctrine of creation typically misinterprets how mainline Christians use the word *God*. A good example is Paul Tillich's understanding of creation. Appropriating Augustine's notion of time, he wrote that God is not an "existent object or being." [17] That is, we cannot say, "God exists" in the same way we can say "apples exist," or for that matter, "the universe exists." The point of the Christian doctrine of creation is that God is the source of all existence. *God* is how Christians (and Jews and Muslims) name whatever is responsible for the existence of all space-time things and events, including human beings.

So the question is, is the universe totally meaningless or is it *about* something? While the natural sciences may not be able to answer this question, they can bring genuine illumination. The rational basis for this ingeniously ordered universe can be simply taken as given, without further inquiry. Or can it be seen as the manifestation of something deeper and more significant. Science neither proves nor disproves the existence of God; it can only offer circumstantial evidence. Each of us must decide for ourselves. Nor can science be religion. But by incorporating spirituality within a scientific framework, the real spiritual needs of human beings can be reconciled with the tenets of our scientific age. Consequently, for Christian theological reflection the problem is how to conceive the possibility of divine action in the universe that does not entail suspending the laws of nature that God created. To the question of how to conceive divine action I will offer some suggestions at the end of this chapter.

EVOLUTIONARY CHALLENGES TO
CHRISTIAN THEOLOGICAL REFLECTION

Among biologists, it is agreed that Charles Darwin's greatest discovery is that adaptation and diversity among living organisms can be explained as an orderly natural process of change over time governed by natural laws organizing matter in motion without reference to divine action. But Darwin was also confronted by a real problem as he wrote *Origin of Species* and its six revised editions. A version of Aquinas's argument

17. Tillich, *Systematic Theology*, 1:235–92.

by design was almost universally held by the "natural philosophers" in Darwin's day; it was popularized by William Paley. Darwin had read Paley's *Natural Theology* while an undergraduate at Cambridge University and found it much to his liking, but by the time he began his five-year voyage around the world on the Beagle as a naturalist, collecting a huge number of insects, birds, plants, and other animals for further study after his return to England, he had changed his mind.

Paley possessed extensive and accurate biological knowledge, as detailed and precise as possible in the mid-nineteenth century. His book is a sustained "argument by design" that claims that the living world supplies evidence that it was created by an omnipotent and omniscient creator. Paley's core thesis was that "there cannot be a design without a designer; contrivance without contriver; order without choice; means suitable to an end, and executing their office in accomplishing that end, without the end ever having been contemplated."[18] Repeatedly, he argued that only an omnipotent and omniscient deity could account for the astonishing complexity of biological processes. Thus just as someone finding a watch on a beach can reasonably conclude that a watchmaker exists, so the complex structure of the human eye can only be explained by the existence of a deity who designed it.

Darwin accepted the notion that organisms are "designed," but not by a creator. He wrote that inherited adaptive variations useful to the survival of species in their particular environments are most likely to appear in organisms. When these adaptations occur, the odds for an organism's survival increase over those organisms in the same species that do not have these adaptations. Those organisms that survive pass on reproductively their adaptive variation to future generations, while members of a species that have not adapted die off. Darwin called this process "natural selection." If enough favorable adaptations are passed on reproductively to new generations over time, the original species will become extinct and be replaced by a new species suitable for survival in its particular environment. In short, evolution is a process of natural selection that "designs" all organisms relative to their environments.

However, Darwin was not clear about how natural selection occurred. It was the rediscovery in 1900 of Gregor Mendel's theory of heredity that joined genetics with evolutionary theory to explain the mechanism of natural selection. Today evolutionary biology is for-

---

18. Paley, *Natural Theology*, cited in Ayala, "The Evolution of Life," 25.

mulated in genetic and statistical terms as differential reproduction, a form of evolutionary theory often referred to by nonscientists as "new-Darwinism." According to the majority contemporary interpretation, natural selection causes some genes and genetic combinations to have higher probabilities of being transmitted than their alternatives. These genetic units will become more common in subsequent generations as their alternatives become less common.

This means that natural selection over time is a statistical bias in the relative rate of the reproduction of alternative genes. In this way, natural selection acts like a filter that eliminates most harmful genetic variations while retaining beneficial ones. But natural selection is much more than a negative process because it also generates novelty by increasing the probability of otherwise extremely improbable genetic combinations through genetic mutation. Natural selection is a creative process in the sense that while it does not "create" the entities upon which it operates, it does produce adaptively functional genetic combinations in living organisms that could have not existed in any other way.

The most troubling aspect of evolutionary biology for theological reflection is that there is no foresight in the operation of natural selection, nor does natural selection operate according to some preconceived plan. It is a strictly impersonal, natural process that emerges from the interaction of the properties of the physical-chemical interactions at play in biological processes. Natural selection might *seem* to have purposefulness because it is contextualized by environmental factors. That is, which organisms reproduce most effectively depends on which genetic variations they posses are useful in the place and time where organisms live. Natural selection does not "anticipate" the environments of living organisms, but drastic environmental changes may be too rapid for an organism's adaptation. Species extinction is a common result of natural selection; 99 percent of all species that have ever lived on Earth have become extinct. Natural selection does not "strive" to produce predetermined kinds of organisms, but only organisms that are adapted to their particular environments.

Consequently, evolutionary biology's challenge to Christian theological reflection involves

- the nature of biblical authority
- the historicity of the biblical creation narratives

- the meaning of Adam's fall from grace
- the nature and scope of God's activity in the universe
- all natural theology, particularly the argument from design
- what it means for human beings to be created in the image of God
- the ultimate grounds of moral value

Because it was easy to set up a contradiction on each of these points between ostensibly "scientific" and ostensibly "religious" points of view, Darwin's theory soon came to symbolize a continual conflict in which militant secularists as well as militant Christian fundamentalists still like to wage war. So from the perspective of science-religion dialogue, the question is, do the methods of science have relevance to the implications of evolution for beliefs bout God, historical progress, and human ethics? The very fact that support from science was, and still is, claimed for such divergent views should make us think harder before we draw conclusions.

A biological concept, natural selection, has been variously converted into an argument for theism, atheistic materialism, or free-market capitalism, each of which must be defended as a philosophical interpretation rather than a scientific conclusion. Similarly, considerable ambiguity emerges in any attempt to derive ethical norms, as in social biology, or scientific justifications for notions of historical progress, on the basis of evolutionary evidence alone. Today the relation of evolution to ethics continues to be of great interest, but there is greater awareness of the difference between a scientific theory and its extension into a universal explanatory scheme or an all-embracing worldview. The nineteenth century taught us the dangers that arise when theologians too easily step out of their methodology and interfere in scientific investigations and conclusions, or when scientists too readily step out of scientific methods to adjudicate theological questions.

The "God of the gaps" has been displaced in biology after Darwin, just as it had been in physics after Laplace. Biological changes are now accounted for by random variation and natural selection. We have Darwin to thank for finally making it clear that God is neither a secondary cause operating on the same level as natural forces nor a means for filling gaps in the scientific theories. How, then, should theologians reflect on divine action, since the heart of Christian faith is that God has acted within the conditions of historical space-time, particularly in the life, death, and resurrection of the historical Jesus as the Christ; and that God continues acting to draw all things and events to a final fulfillment called the *basileia theou*: the kingdom (or in a more contemporary interpretation) the commonwealth of God?

COSMOLOGY, EVOLUTION, AND DIVINE ACTION

From the perspective of process theology, all scientific descriptions of the physical structures of existence will generate boundary questions that necessarily constrain how theologians should reflect on how God can be active in the universe. Furthermore, as scientific theories change, so will the constraints placed on Christian theological reflection. For example, quantum theory, because of the indeterminacy of microsystems it entails, has attracted much attention for the premise that if God is active in all events, then God must be involved in the most fundamental of events that occur at the quantum level. Quantum mechanics is not predictive in the same sense as classical mechanics. While the trajectory of a rocket can be predicted with precise accuracy, the location or spin-rate of an electron cannot. Accordingly, Robert John Russell argues that this indeterminacy constitutes a "causal joint" whereby God can influence events in the macroworld without violating the laws of nature that God created.[19] However, as with all speculation of this sort, there exist problems: it is not clear how God could influence the behavior of electrons and atomic nuclei, or if God in fact did, how this would influence macrosystems. As Phillip Hefner argues, "we ought to resist the temptation to move too easily from quantum-talk to God-talk."[20]

According to Arthur Peacocke, intuitions based on physics and biology make it reasonable for Christians to affirm that a God exists who is: (1) one and undergoes unfathomable richness of experience; (2) supremely rational; (3) a sustainer and faithful preserver; (4) a continual creator of an anthrop universe;[21] (5) purposeful; (6) always in process of

19. Russell, "Finite Creation," 291–326.

20 Hefner, "Editorial," 467–68.

21. The anthropic principle is a cosmological theory that asserts that the four physical forces that govern the universe—the electromagnetic force, the strong force, the weak force, and gravity—are so finely balanced that the universe seems tuned for human life, which implies that the universe must be inhabited by beings like us. Or restated differently, life like ours somehow constrains the fundamental physical forces

becoming; (7) able to experience joy and delight; (8) the source of the interplay between indeterminacy and law; (9) self-limited, omnipotent, and omniscient; (10) vulnerable, self-emptying, and self-giving love; and (11) suffering, because God experiences the suffering of all sentient beings, just as God experiences the joys of all sentient beings.[22] But it must be noted that while "intuitions based on physics and biology" provide sufficient reasons for affirming the existence of God, they do not prove the existence of God. The sciences can neither prove nor disprove God's existence.

Some theologians have appropriated chaos theory in their reflection on divine action. The chaotic behavior of many physical systems might offer a top-down, holistic mechanism by which God can interact with the world. According to John Polkinghorne, God acts through influencing dynamic patterns through input of what Polkinghorne calls "active information."[23] But the issue here is that scientific explanations of the behavior of chaotic systems are based on deterministic mathematical equations of nonlinear systems. For such systems to possess the sort of openness needed to create a "causal joint" through which God can interact with the universe, it is necessary to assume that these equations reflect a more subtle reality than the deterministic reality they describe. Polkinghorne admits that the details of this more subtle reality, being God, cannot be spelled out.[24]

The issue is causation. How can God "cause" any event, either as the creator of the universe or as an actor somehow involved in physical events in the universe? In his theological reflection on this question, Arthur Peacocke draws upon chaos theory, systems theory, and thermodynamics, which over the past fifty years have revealed the role of top-down causation in many physical systems. For example, according to the second law of thermodynamics, in isolated systems undergoing irreversible processes far from equilibrium, the entropy or disorder within such a system always increases. This is the physical reason that no system, including the universe of life forms and the universe itself, is permanent. But simultaneously there also emerge new, more ordered or "organized systems" from systems undergoing entropy. This means

of the universe. See Murphy and Ellis, *On the Moral Nature*, 51–53.

22. Peacocke, *Theology for a Scientific Age*, 102.

23. Polkinghorne, "The Metaphysics of Divine Action," 147–56.

24. Ibid., 153–54.

that in far-from-equilibrium, nonlinear, open systems matter displays a potential for self-organization and is capable bringing new forms into existence by the operation of internal forces and properties, but now operating under the constraints afforded by their being incorporated into a new system, whose properties as a whole have to be taken into account.

That is, changes in the lower microscopic levels of a physical system occur because of top-down causal influences. For example, the molecules of a cell are what they are because of their incorporation into the cell's system as a whole, the organ of which the cell is a part, and ultimately the entire body of a living organism. The whole (the cell) constrains or sets the boundary conditions of the bottom-up action of its constituent parts (the cells' quarks, atoms, and molecules). So the whole cannot be reduced to, and therefore entirely explained by, its lower-level constituent parts.

Of course, theological language is always symbolic, especially when one is reflecting on God. But Peacocke appropriates the scientific fact of bottom-up and top-down causal interdependence to reflect on how God's action in the universe from the big bang singularity and God's subsequent interaction with the universe is possible. Just as the human body sets the boundary condition for the functioning of it individual cells, one may metaphorically think of the universe with all its constituent parts as the "body" of God.[25] The universe is the kind of universe it is because of the way it is constrained by the exquisite balance between the four physical forces holding it together, beginning at Planck time, in such a way that life on Earth began to evolve four billion years ago. The universe is constrained to be the kind of universe it is because God, as the boundary condition of the universe, is immanent "in, with, and under" all things and events at every moment of space-time—just as the evolution of Earth's life forms are constrained by the boundary conditions set by the particular physics of this universe in their individual environmental contexts.

Peacocke's theology is not pantheist, but panentheist. Although he resisted process theology, his views are in fact deeply influenced by Whitehead. As a Christian, he thought that God's eternal selfhood

---

25. Peacocke does not go as far as Sallie McFague, because he thinks this notion runs the risk of ignoring Christian experience of God's nature as transcendent to the universe that God crates, much like an artist transcends a work of art yet incarnates his or her intention and design into a work of art. See McFague, *Models of God*, 69–77.

(Whitehead's "primordial nature of God") always transcends the universe, in much the same way that an artist expresses his or her selfhood in a painting or musical composition while remaining ontologically distinct from the work of art. Nevertheless, God's interaction with the universe affects God (Whitehead's "consequent nature of God") and conditions how God acts in the universe, just as an artist's creative actions affect the artist. The universe as "God's body" does not mean that God's reality is exhausted by or reducible to physical properties of the universe.

Of course, all Christian theologians believe that God created the universe and continually guides the course of the universe's history. This history includes life's evolutionary history. In his explanation of divine action, Peacocke draws on the experimental evidence of biology and the notion of "emergence," the view that new phenomena are not reducible to the subsystems on which they depend, and that newly evolved realities in turn exercise causal influence on the parts out of which they arise. In this sense, according to Peacocke, God engages in top-down, or "whole-part," interaction with the universe, so that divine action is indirect, occurring through a chain of levels acting in a "downward" way.[26]

Catholic process theologian John Haught follows a different direction than Peacocke does. His thesis is that the primary challenge of evolution to Christian faith lies in interpretations of scientific conclusions that uncritically assume the reductionisms of materialist metaphysics, a position often referred to as "scientism." Still, Haught thinks that evolutionary biology is a challenge to all religious traditions because all claim that there exists some point or purpose to the universe, that the cosmos is enshrouded in meaning and purpose to which human beings should surrender.[27] Given the cruel, wasteful, hit-and-miss way in which evolution works, is it feasible to think of the universe as grounded in an ordering principle to which any ideas about the Sacred point? Specifically, for Christian theological reflection, is it feasible that a process that impersonally "creates" the vast complexity of Earth's life forms through the random interplay of chance and necessity over time through natural selection, all without meaning or the need for a sustaining designer, leaves any room for Christian faith in God?

26. Peacocke, *Theology for a Scientific Age*, chap. 11.
27. Haught, *God after Darwin*, 9.

Yet, Haught continues, even as evolution challenges Christian faith and practice, the same challenge presents opportunities for the creative transformation of contemporary Christian theological reflection. Haught names this creatively transformed theology "evolutionary theology," which involves six themes reformulated in light of his dialogue with evolutionary biology: (1) creation, (2) eschatology, (3) revelation, (4) grace, (5) divine power, and (6) redemption.[28]

Traditionally, *creation* is understood as "original creation" (*creatio origina*), "ongoing" or "continual creation" (*creatio continua*), and "new creation" or the "fulfillment of creation" (*creatio nova*). Prior to the cosmological discoveries of physics and the discoveries of biological evolution, continuing creation and the fulfillment of creation were not given much attention by theologians. "Creation meant that God did something 'in the beginning,' which, when pushed to extremes, leads to deism, or the view that God created the universe and then left it to run its own course according to the laws of nature God created "in the beginning."

However, the scientific facts discovered by evolutionary biology now allow theologians to apprehend an ongoing and constantly new reality because, in a constantly changing universe where life is continually evolving, every day is the dawn of a new creation. That is, evolution allows theology to conclude that an originally instantaneous universe is scientifically and theologically incoherent. Moreover, the universe is an imperfect universe, where great suffering is demanded as the price of life itself. Evil and suffering are the dark side of the universe's continuing creation. Creation of any sort cannot occur without suffering. For this reason, Christian faith involves hope for a future eschatological completion of creation.

Eschatology is a form of theological reflection focused on what human beings might hope for as ultimate fulfillment. Haught argues that in an evolutionary context, humanity's hope for final fulfillment must be situated in the wider context of the ongoing creation of the universe. That is, "after Darwin," we can trust that the universe is moving toward a future that includes the entire sweep of evolution. This was also the view of Pierre Teilhard de Chardin, although Haught does not employ Teilhard's "Omega Point" in referring to the universe's final fulfillment.

---

28. For a fuller account of these themes, see ibid., 37–43.

But Haught believes that evolution fits quite well into the framework of biblical eschatology.

Haught further argues that evolution aids theology in reformulating the idea of revelation. Revelation is not the communication of special propositional information from a divine source to specific persons, but rather the communication of God's own selfhood to all human and non-human life. So understood, revelation is a process whereby "the infinite" pours God's self fully and without reservation into creation wherever creation occurs. Such revelatory outpouring is an expression of God's character as love. But the fulfillment of God's character as love cannot be apprehended instantaneously by a finite cosmos. Revelation can take place only in increments because a finite universe can only adapt itself to its infinite source by gradual expansion and ongoing self-transcendence, the external manifestations of which might appear to scientists as cosmic and biological evolution.

A theology of grace also makes intelligible the randomness of natural selection. The doctrine of grace affirms that God loves the universe in all its various expressions and life forms unconditionally, with no strings attached. Love does not absorb, annihilate, or force itself on the beloved. God as love longs for the beloved to become independent. Consequently, a central intuition of Christian faith is that God loves the universe so that God's grace entails letting go of the universe itself. Only a relatively independent universe allowed to be itself can be intimate with God. Theologically interpreted, then, evolution is a story of struggle for expansive freedom for all living things and events in the presence of God's self-giving grace. Seen from this point of view, randomness is an essential feature of any universe created by a gracious God.

Process theology is more attentive to evolutionary biology on the question of divine power than evangelical and fundamentalist traditions of theology in the way that it conceives how deeply God is involved with a universe wherein life on Earth meanders, experiments, strives, fails, and sometimes succeeds. In agreement with the majority of process theologians, Haught thinks of divine power as "the capacity to influence" so that "persuasive love," rather than coercion, is the defining character of God's power. God does not magically force things and events to fulfill divine intentions in miraculous ways that contradict the laws of nature that God created. A coercive deity is one that immature minds may wish for and that scientific skeptics most often have in mind when they assert that evolutionary biology has destroyed theism. But given the nature of God's character as love, God wills the independence of the universe, rather than being a Calvinistic despot who controls every event through willing every outcome.

Haught also upholds process theology's claim that a universe given the freedom to become more and more autonomous, creating itself in the process and eventually attaining human consciousness and freedom, has much more integrity and value than any conceivable universe determined in every aspect by an omnipotent designer. Furthermore, divine power interpreted, as coercive will is incompatible not only with human freedom but also with the pre-human spontaneity that allowed life to evolve into something other than God. Evolution occurs because a God of love is also the source of not only the universe's order, but also its novelty. It is the introduction of novelty into the universe that makes evolution necessary. Because God is more interested in novelty than in preserving the status quo, God's will is best understood as the maximization of cosmic beauty and intensity of experience for all sentient beings. Or in Haught's words, "the epic of evolution is the world's response to God's longing that it strive for richer ways of realizing aesthetic intensity."[29] By offering ever new and rich possibilities to the universe, God sustains and continually creates the universe. Or as Whitehead wrote, God is more interested in "adventure" than in preserving the status quo.[30]

Finally, again drawing on process theology, Haught argues that evolutionary biology supports a revised Christian understanding of redemption. The question is, given the perpetual perishing that is structurally part of all cosmic processes because of the second law of thermodynamics, for what can one reasonably hope. Haught's answer is the same as that given in the New Testament, particularly 1 Corinthians 15: God is infinitely responsive to the universe wherever life occurs in the universe. Because God's nature is love, the polar side of which is justice, like any lover, God "feels" of "prehends" the universe and wherever life occurs in the universe by taking it into God's self. God responds to the universe accordingly, so that every thing and event is "saved" by being taken eternally into God's own feelings for the universe. Even as all

---

29. Ibid., 69.

30. See Whitehead, *Adventures of Ideas*, 252–96, for his argument that God's relation to the universe is more accurately conceived as an "adventure" that "lures" all creation to new levels of intensity of experience.

things and events are the achievement of the physics in interdependence with biological evolution, so all things and events abide permanently within the everlasting compassion of God.[31]

THE DIFFICULT PATH

Ted Peters notes that anyone practicing theological reflection has entered a difficult path.[32] No theologian follows the easy route allegedly taken by the scientific community: remain skeptical until empirical proof requires belief. Perhaps in my case I have chosen the difficult path because I have been victimized by a tradition based on revelation. I have a strong hunch that in the historical Jesus as the Christ, the transcendent has invaded the immanent. The mysterious and unfathomable has redefined what is natural and understandable. Yet God's entry into the finitude of the human condition and the universe's history has done us few, if any, favors. What we might desire from revelation is a wisdom that opens out toward the visible landscape of the transcendent. But the window is closed, and, like a mirror, turns us back to look on our own mundane reality. Christian revelation reminds us *that* there is a divine reality standing over against our world, but to know exhaustively *what* that divine reality is remains impossible within the boundary conditions of knowledge circumscribed by our experiences. Yet being unable to say "what it is" does prevent us from partially "knowing what it is." So it seems that a theologian's task is make the effort to partially understand what is transcendent in terms of available knowledge of reality, including what is known scientifically.

However, the sciences neither prove nor disprove the existence of God even as the sciences can add much needed reasonableness to Christian faith and understanding. It has always been so from the first century, when its dialogue with Greek natural philosophy contextualized the meaning of Christian faith, until the twenty-first century. It will be so in the future. Of course not all Christians seek dialogue with the natural sciences. It is also true that some scientists and philosophers of science have confused metaphysical materialism with science in their polemics against religion in general and Christian faith in particular. Fundamentalism is not only a Christian sin.

---

31. Ibid., 42.

32. Peters, "Resurrection: The Conceptual Challenge," 297–98.

But while dialogue with the natural sciences provides a context for reasonable Christian theological reflection, it does not provide the fundamental foundations for betting one's life on, that is, for having faith in, God. Faith, particularly Christian faith, should be grounded in knowledge of the physical processes of this universe, but even more important, on wider bodies of aesthetic, moral, and communal experience, on what Joseph Campbell referred to as the "universals of human experience." All human beings in whatever culture in whatever time experience death, hunger, disease, the need for community, love, fear, hope, beauty, and ugliness. It is the universals of human experience, contextualized by our knowledge of the world revealed by the sciences, that sets the boundary conditions (and the resulting cognitive dissonance) for belief in God.

If process theologians are right, and I think they are, God must be an experience contextualized through the universals of human experience before God can be an object of theological reflection. Unless this is the case, whatever words we use will be without content. As mystics of all religious traditions tell us, we need to make sure that the words we use in speaking or writing about God are preceded by, or at least come out of, an experience that is our own. Of course, all reflection on experience is rooted in a particular community—in my case a liberal process theological community that includes a few Lutherans. But any experience of God will be the kind of experience that in some way touches us deeply, perhaps even tosses us from the back of a horse, as it did St. Paul, and it will fill us with wonder and gratitude as it throws our hip out of joint, as it did for Jacob during his wrestling match with God at the River Jabbok (Genesis 32:24–31) Finally, it will be an experience for which there are no adequate words.

So, again following the advice of Christian mystical tradition, I shall conclude this chapter with a *theologia negavita* or "negative theology" by reflecting on what God is not, given my understanding of the historical Jesus as the Christ contextualized by current scientific descriptions of the natural processes of the world God continually creates from the first moment of the big bang.

First, God is not a cosmic moralist. This notion, at its worst, imagines God as a divine lawgiver and judge who has proclaimed an arbitrary set of moral rules, keeps records of offenders, and punishes them accordingly. In its less legalistic interpretation, God is most fundamentally concerned with the development of moral attitudes. This makes primary for God what is secondary for human beings, and limits the scope of the intrinsic import of human beings as perhaps the only beings capable of moral attitudes. I deny the existence of this sort of God.

Second, God is not an unchanging, passionless absolute reality. This notion derives from the Greeks, who maintained that "perfection" entailed complete "immutability," or lack of change. The concept of impassibility stresses that God must be completely unaffected by any other reality and must lack all passion or emotional response to beings in the world. This notion means that God is not really related to the world, although the world is externally related to God because the existence of the world requires the existence of a deity who created it. But God is wholly independent the world, and the world's relation to God is purely external to God. I deny the existence of this sort of God.

Third, God is not an all-controlling power. This idea suggests God determines every event that has happened, now happens, and will happen in the universe. So, for example, when someone unexpectedly dies, it is often asked, "Why?" meaning "Why did God choose to take this life at this time?" Also, when destructive natural disasters occur, such as hurricanes, earthquakes, or tidal waves, insurance companies often speak of "acts of God," mostly because they are looking for a way out of paying their customers for their losses. On the positive side, persons who survive a natural disaster while hundreds of other people lose their lives, might regard this as an act of God to explain how they survived against the odds. But what kind of God spares some while allowing others to die? I deny the existence of this sort of God.

Fourth, God is not a miracle worker. In contemporary English usage the word *miracle* means that God occasionally interrupts the orderly working of the laws of nature God creates to cause events to happen that would not otherwise occur. But in the Tanakh and the New Testament, such events are not called miracles but "signs and wonders," "mighty deeds," "wonders and powers," or simply "signs" in the Gospel of John.[33] Such events, while unusual, were regarded by first- and second-century Christians as part of the natural order of things.

But events called miracles, that interrupt the laws of nature to achieve a purpose that God desires at a particular time and place, implies

---

33. In Hebrew, 'otothai va mophethai and in Greek, semei ka terata. See Exod 7:5; Deut 6:22; Neh 9:10; Ps 135:9; Jer 32:21; Dan 4:2, 6:27; Mark 6:2; the Gospel of John; and 2 Cor 12:12.

that God capriciously interrupts the orders of God's creation in some arbitrary fashion. If people of faith have experienced something like "signs and wonders," they have not experienced a miracle but an extraordinary event allowed by the laws of nature God created and maintains. For one thing, a God of miracles is not a dependable God who loves all things and events universally. For another, a God of miracles makes the problem of evil impossible to resolve. On what basis does God intervene in one person's life and not in another's? So if an extraordinary event like the resurrection of the historical Jesus or the cure of a human being with an "incurable disease" actually happened, it is because the laws governing the universe permit it to happen even if we cannot identify the reason it happened. I deny the existence of this sort of God.

Fifth, God is not a sanctioner of the status quo. This is a strong tendency in all monotheistic religious traditions and is supported in the notion of God as an all-controlling power. Also, the idea that God is an unchanging Absolute suggests God's creation of an unchangeable order for the world. Notions that God is a controlling power suggest that the present order of the universe exists because God wills its existence. In this case, faithful obedience to God means preserving the status quo, even if the status quo is oppressive. I deny the existence of this sort of God.

Sixth, God's nature is not masculine. Feminist liberation theology has demonstrated how deeply images and concepts of God are sexually one sided and need to include feminine images. Not only has theology understood the three "persons" of the Trinity (Father, Son, Holy Spirit) as male, but Christian theological tradition has reinforced these male images of God through the classical idea that God is totally active, independent, controlling, and completely lacking in receptiveness and responsiveness. According to these ideas, God seems like the perfect archetype of the dominant, inflexible, unemotional, completely independent "strong male" of patriarchal societies throughout the world. I deny the existence of this sort of God.

Of course, negative or positive God-talk is inadequate because whenever we say anything negative or positive about God, we always crash into the cognitive dissonance of boundary constraints, just as scientists crash into boundaries that engender cognitive dissonance about the physical processes at play in the universe. Theological reflection, like scientific reflection, is, at best, symbolic, never literal. In koan-like fashion, all talk about God, positively or negatively, is a "finger pointing at the moon." My dialogue with Buddhism has taught me that we should never cling to doctrines, symbols, or ideas about anything, because to the degree that we do (the moment we confuse the "finger with the moon"), we never apprehend the moon as it is. Cling to positive or negative ideas about God, and you have only a positive or negative idea about God.

Still, something can be said. Buddhists talk positively about Awakening, nonself, and Emptying even as they say that nothing can actually be said about Awakening, nonself, and Emptying. Just shut up, meditate, and experientially realize Awakening, nonself, and Emptying. Similarly in Christian experience, God is not merely transcendent but immanent in all space-time things and events since the big bang. So Christian mystics advice us to stop the ideological clutter in our heads, to shut up, and to "enter the Silence," as Thomas Merton phrased it, and encounter a divine reality that can never be reduce to negative or positive words, doctrines, definitions, or symbols taken literally. But in agreement with Zen teachers like Masao Abe and other members of the Kyoto school, even Thomas Merton wrote books about what cannot be reduced to words and letters.

So any deity that is *completely* transcendent—in addition that it would be contradictory to even speak about such a deity—would be a superfluous, if not a perverse, hypothesis. A completely transcendent God would deny immanence at the same time that it would destroy human transcendence. The divine mystery is ineffable—its transcendence and immanence—, and no negative or positive discourse can completely describe it. Theological reflection, in the end, is always paradoxical because theologians are always talking about what cannot, in the final analysis, be completely said.

Keeping in mind, then, the paradoxical nature of all talk about God, I shall conclude this chapter with some brief positive God-talk that reflects my current understanding of what God is not. The source of this more positive language reflects my understanding of the New Testament (particularly the Synoptic Gospels and the Prologue to the Gospel of John) and my dialogue with the world's religions (particularly Buddhism, Judaism, and Islam), and contemporary science-religion dialogue, all joined with the resources of process philosophical theology. In the following chapter, I shall try to interrelate the positive God-talk of this section with specific themes of Christian theological reflection about the relationship between the historical Jesus and the Christ of faith and practice.

For two thousand years, Christian faith has held that the basic character of God is best described as love. But the meaning of the statement "God is love" is not particularly self-evident in classical Christian thought, particularly when joined with images of God as a masculine cosmic moralist, an unchanging, passionless absolute reality, and an all-controlling power that sanctions the status quo. In Charles Hartshorne's version of process theism, sometimes called dipolar theism, God's nature is constituted by two poles or aspects: God's abstract essence and God's concrete actuality. God's abstract essence is eternal, absolute, independent, and unchangeable. It includes those abstract attributes that characterize God's existence at every moment of space-time. So, for example, to affirm that God is omniscient means that in every knowable moment of God's life God knows everything that is knowable at that moment. But God does not know events before they happen, for the future is empty of content to be known other than by anticipation. Like human beings in "the image of God," God can anticipate the future but does not know the future before it happens. God's concrete actuality is temporal, relative, dependent, and constantly changing. In each moment of God's life there are new, unforeseen happenings in the world that only then have become knowledge. This is so because God's concrete knowledge of the world is dependent upon decisions made by worldly things and events. God's knowledge is always relativized, because it is interdependent with all actual events happening in the universe past and present.

Whitehead's conception of divine dipolarity is not identical with Hartshorne's. Whitehead distinguished between God's "primordial nature "and God's "consequent nature." The term *consequent nature* is largely identical with what Hartshorne called God's "concrete actuality." Since the consequent nature of God is fully actual, the term *consequent* makes the same point as Hartshorne's term *relative*, namely, that God as fully actual and responsively receptive of every space-time thing and event. It is God's primordial nature that offers every space-time thing and event an "initial aim" to actualize the best possibilities open to it, given its particular concrete situation. But God's initial aim does not become automatically a thing or event's "subjective aim," which is a product of its own decision. An event may choose to actualize God's initial aim for it; but it may also choose from among other real possibilities open to it according to its own subjective aim to achieve its own ideal of "satisfaction." That is, God seeks to persuade each occasion toward those possibilities for its own existence that would be best for it. But God does not control a finite occasion's choices for its own self-actualization. Consequently, God's creative activity involves risk, and since God is not in complete control of the universe, the occurrence of evil and great suffering entailed by biological evolution, is not, as Haught argues, incompatible with God's love for all creatures.

Since persuasion, not divine control, is God's way of doing things in the universe, this is the way we should seek to achieve our goals. Much of the tragedy in the course of human history has been caused by the idea that to control others is to share in divinity. Although classical theology affirmed that God is essentially love, God's love was subordinated to God's power. Even though the life, death, and resurrection of the historical Jesus, as well as his message, should have led theologians to back off from Aristotle and to define God's power in terms of God's love, this did not happen. Power, in the sense of controlling domination, remained—and still remains for most people—the essential defining attribute of God's nature. Consequently, human control of things, events, and other persons took on an added sense of satisfaction that comes from participating in an attribute understood to be divine.

Process theology's understanding of God as love is in harmony with an insight we gain from our own experiences: when we truly love others we do not seek to control them. We do not seek to pressure them with promises of rewards or threats of punishment. Rather, we try to persuade them to actualize those possibilities that they themselves will find intrinsically rewarding. We do this by providing an environment that helps open up new, intrinsic possibilities. If it is true that human beings are "created in God's image," why should God's love not be reflected in the ways human beings truly love?

5

"Who Do You Say That I Am?"

ACCORDING TO KAREN ARMSTRONG, theological reflection is a species of poetry, which, when read quickly or encountered in a hubbub of noise, makes no sense.[1] This is so because theological reflection lives at the boundaries of experience and intellect and, like the words and rhythms of a poem, points beyond itself to truths that are elusive, that resist words and conceptualizations. Like the sciences, theology encounters boundaries and the resulting cognitive dissonance that push toward new meanings. This is historically the case with the central claim of Christian faith and practice: two thousand years ago human beings encountered God incarnated in the life, death, and resurrection of a Jewish peasant. Certainly not all that God is, but nevertheless God within the conditions of historical existence. Christians have been trying to figure out the meaning Jesus's question to the Apostle Peter ever since: "But who do you say that I am?" (Mark 8:29).

What does confessing the historical Jesus is the Christ of faith mean? While it turns out that the Apostles' and Nicene Creeds are confessed by the majority of Christians to be the best answers to Jesus's question, there has always existed disagreement about what these confessions mean. Add to this mix many conservative evangelical and fundamentalist traditions, it is empirically evident that there has always existed a plurality of confessions of who the historical Jesus was, and is.

Biography has always been the first clue in theological reflection. According to Jesus's biography in the Synoptic Gospels, he apparently taught mostly in parables that were often so bewilderingly elusive that his disciples would ask for further clarification of their meaning. According to Mark, Jesus "did not speak to the crowds without a

---

1 Armstrong, *The Spiral Staircase*, 284.

parable, but privately to his own disciples he explained everything" (Mark 4:33–34). Jesus's parables are metaphors that do not contract into simple demonstrations, but broaden continually to take on fresh meanings and connotations. Parables invite their hearers into familiar situations, but finally veer off into the unfamiliar, shattering their own realism by insisting on further reflection and inquiry. Whenever I read Jesus's parables, I always have the uneasy feeling that *I* am being interpreted as I interpret them. In this sense, Jesus's parables resemble Zen koans in which we are left hanging until we find illumination through deep meditation, as in the concluding lines of this parable in the Gospel of Luke: "For all who exalt themselves will be humbled, and all who humble themselves will be exalted" (18:14).

It is theological reflection on Jesus's parables that leads to the central christological claim of Christian faith and practice: the reality of God is biographically incarnated in the historical Jesus—the divine word or Logos incarnated in human terms and engaged with just those issues of suffering and mysteries of meaning that most bewilder and oppress human beings. So I shall begin with an experience from my biography before delving into my particular understanding of the incarnation.

The claim that God incarnated God's self in the life of a human being named Jesus of Nazareth is *not* a claim that God has not incarnated God's self elsewhere in the universe or in other human beings. But in the biography of Jesus of Nazareth, Christians claim to have encountered God. Certainly not all that God is, but nevertheless God. From the viewpoint of process theology, there has never been a time when God has not incarnated God's initial aim that each thing and event achieve the most intense harmonious self-fulfillment of which it is capable, much like an artist incarnates part of his or her self in a poem or a painting. Consider the Prologue to the Gospel of John: "In the beginning was the Word, and the Word was with God, and the Word was God. He was in the beginning with God. All things came into being through him, and without him not one thing came into being. What has come into being was life, and the life was the light of all people. The light shines in the darkness, and the darkness did not overcome it" (John 1:1–5).[2]

John's Prologue has always amazed me. With little explanation, the writer of John appropriates Hebraic creation traditions and mixes these

---

2. All citations from the Bible are from *Lutheran Study Bible, Revised Standard Version.*

with Greek philosophical traditions that allow the writer to proclaim that the transcendent God has always been relationally immanent, and thereby accessible, in creation, since the first moment of what we now call the big bang, and, counting back from our time, particularly accessible in historical space-time two thousand years ago, incarnated in the life, death, and resurrection of a particular human being located within a particular culture within a particular Jewish tradition. Or in the koan-like brevity of Philippians, the historical Jesus as the Christ, "though he was in the form of God, did not regard equality with God as something to be exploited, but emptied himself, taking the form of a slave . . . and became obedient to the point of death, even death on a cross" (Philippians 2:5–6).

This is quite a claim. No other religious tradition makes one quite like it: God, who is absolutely transcendent, is also absolutely immanent, and thereby accessible in nature and the rough-and-tumble of historical existence; not only "in the beginning" (John 1:1) but here and now and in the future; not only "dwelling among us" (John 1:14) incarnated in a single human being two thousand years ago; but here and now and also in the future—"in, with, and under" nature and human beings. So I sometimes wonder if Christians are sufficiently aware of conditions. If what I think the writer of John is saying is an accurate interpretation, we should follow Annie Dillard's suggestions and have ushers "lash us to our pews," or we should fasten ourselves to our meditation cushions. As Dillard says, in church "we should all be wearing crash helmets."[3] If God was truly among us in the historical Jesus who is also the Christ of faith, then (to follow Dillard's line of thinking) New Testament scholars should tell their students, "Hold on, boys and girls," or to take off on something Bette Davis once said in *All about Eve*, "Fasten your seatbelts. It's going to be . . . bumpy."[4]

Permit me to describe just how bumpy the ride can be.[5] I think I first began to understand the immanent accessibility of the transcendent God in nature while backpacking alone on the Olympic Peninsula in Washington State about twenty years ago. I followed a game trail through opaque, self-concealing forest that broke onto a boulder and driftwood

3. Dillard, "An Expedition to the Pole," 52.

4. Mankiewicz, *All about Eve*.

5. What follows is a partial description of a personal experience I first recounted in Ingram, *Wrestling with the Ox*, 57–58.

covered beach. It was an old trail, mostly taken over by deer on their way to a nearby creek that emptied onto the beach. Hemlock and red cedar loomed overhead from a floor matted with feathery moss, as if pulled up by invisible wires into the coastal fog.

I walked onto the beach into a setting sun that painted everything orange—ocean waves breaking hard on rocks, forest crowding the beach, fog hanging on the trees like gray cotton wool, light rain dimpling the creek and losing itself in the breakers. Sharp sounds popped across the rocks on my left, and I saw two elk—a bull and a cow—run as if on cue over a small grass-covered dune. My thoughts drifted away from the forest, the earth, the sea, the light, and the elk, and focused inside myself. I suddenly became sharply conscious of my own breathing—a cool, fresh sensation of energy rushing from the life of the earth into my chest, and then warm, moist air, brushing soft as a kiss against my face as I exhaled.

And then I knew: every breath I take draws the life of creation into myself. I breathe in soft, saturated exhalations of red cedar and salmonberry bush, fireweed and wood fern, osprey and black bear, martin and blacktail deer, salmon, and raven. I breathe in the same particles of air that form songs in the territorial calls of ravens and give voice to humpback whales, that lift the wings of bald eagles, and buzz in the hum of insects. I breathe in the earth, pass it on, and share it in equal measure with billions of other living creatures. I drink from the creek and it becomes me; and like the elk and the gulls hovering in the westerly wind, I bring the earth inside myself as food.

The interdependency of God and nature—God's intention that all creatures live in harmonious, interdependent balance—is an expression of God's creative word from the very beginning. It is a reflection of the light of God's love for God's creation, always there, stalking all things, like cougars on the hunt. For how empty and incomplete would creation be without the sights and sound and smells that make life alive: blackbirds quibbling like druids; horses galloping on a soft track; crows sounding like they're choking on bark; elk bugling like the sound of distant war games; nighthawks making their call, a distinct metallic ping; crickets chirping together like a band of kindergarteners; hungry female mosquitoes making their electric whine; redheaded woodpeckers tapping out their Morse code. And how empty creation would be without the presence and sounds of us: the birth cries of newborn babies, the sounds of human speech, the verbal and auditory pictures of literature and music, the imagination of the visual arts, the abstractions of philosophy and the sciences, the play of children and skillful athletes in competition, the laugher of lovers and friends and colleagues, the pluralism of the world's religions.

Of course, there is pain and great suffering in God's created order. Nature's interdependent balance is maintained through predator-prey relationships—life must eat life to survive. Evolution is also part of God's creation. But pain is often cruel, and cruelty is always a mystery and a waste of pain, even for God. Furthermore, God's gift of freedom allows us to misuse our own creativity in inventive and hideously destructive ways that inflict pain on nature and on our own species. Looked at realistically, human beings seem to be blots on God's creation, because, somehow, we seem not to have worked out the way Genesis 1 says God intended. To understand this, all we need do is look in the mirror when we get up in the morning. The face that pins us there with its double stare reflects the eyes of the most efficient and remorseless predator to have evolved on this planet. God may have intended nature to be balanced, harmonious, and interdependent, but it's also rough in nature, whether in a rainforest or in an urban jungle, where pain and cruelty often mask God's intentions.

And yet there is something else. According to John's use of Hebraic creation traditions in Geneses 1–11, God, the creator of the universe has created us, predators or not—all of us—in God's "own image" by no process of mass production. Each of us is a specially designed reproduction of God's image, which implies there is a special place in creation that only we can fill. We have unique responsibilities before God that cannot be delegated to any other creature. Moreover, we have the capability of understanding God and loving God, which is in principle unique. Apprehending and entering into this unique relationship is first the embarrassment—and then the joy—of every single individual's movements toward personal communion with God and with other creatures. For God's creative word is not only addressed to the world and to creatures in the world in general, but to human beings in particular. It is a word that calls us to the struggle for justice and compassion in human community. It is a call to balance the needs of the human community with the needs of nature. Some have heard this Word; some have occasionally paid attention to it; some have asked it to go away.

Once upon a time, a group of nomadic Hebrews did just that. They heard God's word bellowing on Mount Sinai in thunder and smoke and found it too loud: "All the people saw the thunder and the lightning, and the noise of the trumpet, and the mountain smoking," Exodus 20:19 records. It scared them witless, and they asked Moses to beg God, please, never to speak directly to them again: "Let God not speak to us, or we will die" (20:19). And God, pitying their self-consciousness, agreed to become inaccessible to them. "Go say to the people," God instructed Moses, "'Get into your tents again.'"

It's very difficult to undo our damage and ask God to come back after we have asked God to go away. Still, these Hebrew nomads had a point. As the psalmist wrote, "Who shall ascend the hill of the LORD? Or who shall stand in his holy place?" (Psalm 24:3). The answer is, there is no one but us. There is no one else to send, not a clean hand, nor a pure heart (cf. Psalm 24:4) on the face of the planet, but only us—human beings made in God's image, comforting ourselves with the notion that we have come, like the nomadic Hebrews at Sinai, at an awkward time. But there is not one of us who has—there never has been a generation of men and women who have—lived well for even one day.

Yet some of us have imagined the details of such a well-lived life worthy to ascend to the hill of God, and have described such a life with such grace that we sometimes mistake their visions for history, their visions for description, and fancy that human life has evolved. You learn this by studying any history at all, especially the lives of visionaries and artists. You learn it from Emerson and Yeats and Eliot; you learn it from Picasso and Dali; you learn it from leaders in the struggle against racism and oppression, like Martin Luther King Jr., Mahatma Gandhi, or Thich Nhat Hanh; you learn it from the writer of John's Prologue: we do not, because we cannot, ascend "to the hill of the Lord" by our own self-justifications, because there is no is no hill to ascend; there never has been a hill to ascend to encounter God's creative word. It's the opposite that is the case. God's eternally creative Word comes to us: through creation and—get this!—enfleshed in the historical Jesus of Nazareth two thousand years ago; and now—get this too!—as the Holy Spirit, pouring over us and everything else in nature the way light floods out darkness.

We need to have faith in this Light that has always enfleshed God's creation. As I have written throughout this book, faith is trust. It is never reducible to creeds, theological opinions, doctrines, beliefs *about* God or about the relation between the historical Jesus and God. Specifically Christian faith is trust—betting one's life—that whatever we can learn will lead more fully into the light of God's truth. Even when, at the moment, what we learn seems to take us into darkness and despair, faith does not quit, does not give up, does not intellectually cut and run. In faith, one lets go of one's ideas, does not cling to them (not even to one's ideas of God or the historical Jesus as the Christ), in the confidence that in this way we will see the light of God's creativity that is gracefully spilling over creation like a waterfall, absolutely accessible, in, with, and under everything, closer to us than our own breath.

But personal biography alone is never enough, because dwelling within one's own particular subjective religious experiences only expresses one's subjectivity. Absolutizing one's own experiences also runs the risk of committing what Whitehead called "the fallacy of misplaced concreteness." Also, subjective experiences run the risk of delusion of the sort that too easily confuses one's individual experiences for the whole truth and nothing but the truth. Hindus refer to this tendency as *maya*, or "delusion." One of the lessons I have learned from dialogue with Muslims is in regard to *shirk*, or "idolatry": it is too easy to fool oneself and others with the confusions of partial glimpses of truth for the whole truth. Surrendering (*islām*) to a subjectively experienced "truth" as if it were the whole truth is called "idolatry" in the Qur'an. This is why reason must address private experience within the context of a faith community (in this instance, the Christian community) in dialogue with other religious communities and, wherever possible, with the natural sciences.

In the early church, the "work" of the historical Jesus was understood in two ways. One of the ways St. Paul described faith was "life in Christ," and this can be understood in more contemporary terms as a "field of force" generated by the historical Jesus's life, death, and resurrection. The compilers of Q (the source of Jesus sayings), and the gospel writers who used Q were impressed by the power of Jesus's teaching. Being "in" Christ's "field of force" and hearing "the teachings of the historical Jesus" they thought they heard opened early Christians to the experience of creative transformation.

From the point of view of process philosophy and the natural sciences, the notion of a field of force is not particularly mysterious. Every event pervades its future by anticipating it in relation to its prehension of its past. Of course, the effect of most of these events, including human ones, on the future is negligible. But there are important events whose field of force is not negligible. Such an event is the life of the historical Jesus, and its repeated remembrance through liturgical reenactment in such rituals as baptism and the Eucharist has continued to strengthen its field of force in contemporary times. To participate in a field of force is to conform in some measure to the historical event that generated the field. Accordingly, to be "in Christ," in St. Paul's sense, is to conform one's life to the historical Jesus's life and death. Because the historical Jesus was so open to the processes of creative transformation, to conform to him is to share in that openness.

To genuinely hear the historical Jesus's teaching, as recorded in Q and the Synoptic Gospels, is simultaneously to experience Jesus as the Christ and as creative transformation. Whitehead himself noted how these teachings, just because of their impracticality, create cognitive dissonance in relation to every existing theological and social system. When what the conventional world is inclined to take for granted is rendered suspicious, one is open to creative transformation. This is so because he spoke directly to his hearers about their own experiences. Or as Reinhold Niebuhr noted, Jesus afflicted the comfortable and comforted the afflicted.

Transformation happens because the historical Jesus opens persons to the possibilities of creative transformation that calls for reflecting on how creative transformation was at work in his life. The question is, how was God related to the historical Jesus so that he became the Christ of faith? Was Jesus only a Jewish teacher, or something else? To be sure, all attempts to describe the structure of existence of an individual or community are speculative inferences. Furthermore, description of the structure of Jesus's existence must focus on what current New Testament scholarship regards as his authentic sayings. This scholarship reveals two characteristics of the sayings of Jesus—his parables and specific teachings. First, they express an immediate and undistorted insight into the conditions of human existence. Second, Jesus spoke and acted as if he had a peculiar authority. This claim of authority went far beyond that of the Hebrew prophets, although most of what Jesus said and did is grounded in the prophetic tradition. Jesus's structure of existence seems to have been distinctive in its mode of relating to God.

Classical Christology also asserts God's presence in Jesus, but in a way that entailed an unintentional denial of Jesus's full humanity. This reflects the substance metaphysics of Greek philosophy, which required that if the Logos is present in Jesus, some part of his human nature must be displaced. But from a process perspective, Jesus's relation to God involves no denial of his full humanity. The basis for this affirmation is that every actuality is an occasion of experience, in which other experiences, including the experience of God, are incarnated. So the presence of God in Jesus does not make Jesus an exception to reality in general or to humanity in particular. The problem is how to characterize Jesus's relation to God as distinctive.

One way in which structures of existence can be distinguished is according to the constitution of the integrating center of experience, meaning, the self or *I*. When we are infants, this organizing center is controlled largely by our bodily experiences. But normal adult experiences are constituted by the presence of our personal past, largely through memory. Our experiences are organized in terms of purposes and memories inherited from the past. It is this historical route of experiences that determines our self-identity through time.

But also in all experiences the divine presence is incarnated in the form of God's initial aim for all things and events—what process thinkers, following Whitehead, refer to as "actual occasions of experience." The initial aim from God is what is best for that occasion of experience in every moment of its existence in interdependence with every other occasion in the universe. But there is tension between God's initial aim and an occasion's subjective aim for itself. That is, for most of us the divine presence is experienced as other, occasionally as gracious, often as judgmental or absent.

But in Jesus's authentic sayings, his structure of existence does not reflect this otherness. Instead, Jesus's selfhood seems to be constituted by God's agency as initial aim in union with his own subjective aim and personal past. That is, in the historical Jesus, God's initial aim for him and his subjective aim for himself are, in Buddhist language, "nondual." Or as David Ray Griffin writes, "We may think of Jesus' structure of existence in terms of an 'I' that is co-constituted as much by the divine agency within him as by his own personal past."[6] The normal tensions between God's initial aim and the purposes received from the past

6. Cobb and Griffin, *Process Theology*, 105.

(expressive of our subjective aim to achieve our own individual fulfillment) did not exist in the historical Jesus; Jesus's subjective aim was
conformed to God's initial aim for him. This, in turn, created openness
to God's call in each moment of Jesus's life. Whereas the Christ (Logos)
is incarnated in all things and events, in every human being, the historical Jesus *is* the Christ because God's incarnation constituted his very
selfhood.

Consequently, the historical Jesus was fully human. But for whatever reason, Jesus conformed his subjective aim for himself to God's initial
aim for Jesus, and in so doing he became *the* Christ. One can therefore
affirm that "the Christ" in the form of God's initial aim is incarnated in
all things and events at every moment of space-time: past, present, or
future. But the historical Jesus became "the Christ" by identifying his
subjective aim for himself with God's initial aim for him, or to quote
words he is reported as having said before he was killed, "Not my will,
but your will." This means the historical Jesus was no different than any
other human being because, in the language of the Nicene Creed, he
"was made man." But in the unity of his subjective aim with God's will
(God's initial aim), he was in nondual harmony with the Christ or *Logos*
that is incarnated in all things and events, according to the Prologue to
the Gospel of John.

THE ATONEMENT

Classical theological reflection about human selfhood originated in early
translations of biblical texts through the categories of Greek philosophy,
particularly Platonic, Aristotelian, Neoplatonic, and Stoic thought. Thus
God creates each human being as an embodied soul, so that there are as
many souls as there have been human beings. Each soul is the eternal,
unchanging center of the rational, emotional, and moral experiences of
each human being's self-identity through time. In classical theological
thinking, even today, when a person dies, the soul is released from its
physical embodiment, its final destiny assigned by God according to
its deeds while it was alive; either paradise, an intermediate state called
Purgatory (if one is a Roman Catholic), or permanent punishment in
hell. Of course, there exist numerous themes, variations, and levels of
complexity and sophistication in this classical teaching. But all are open
to two criticisms: (1) they have little, if any, relation to either biblical
images of human selfhood or biblical images of God; and (2) they have

little, if any, relation to how persons actually experience self-identity through time.

Contemporary biblical scholarship consistently demonstrates the nonduality of human selfhood. Nowhere in the Bible do images of human selfhood directly or indirectly assume the existence of a substantially permanent soul or self-entity remaining changelessly self-identical through time. On the contrary, biblical images of human selfhood are holistic and "processive" because the human self is portrayed as a unity of "soul," "body," "flesh," and "spirit" interdependently constituting the whole person throughout the moments of a person's existence until death. Particularly in St. Paul's anthropology, *psyche* ("soul") does not designate a substantial soul-entity, and the word *psyche* is the Greek word for the Hebrew *nephesh*, meaning "life" or "vitality" or "aliveness." The *psyche* is a particular "life" that can be cared for, "saved," judged, or lost. Saint Paul always connects *psyche* with *soma* or "body," which does not merely denote a person's physiological attributes, but rather the whole person—mentally, morally, and physically. We do not *have* bodies; we *are* bodies, animated by "life" until we die. *Soma* and *psyche* are interdependent.

As living, embodied beings, selves are capable of interaction with the environing world as subjects of their own actions. Ideally, our subjective aim for our satisfaction and God's initial aim for us should be nondual, so that our thoughts and actions correspond to what God wills. But St. Paul taught that human selves are so estranged from one another and from God that all selves are at the mercy of "powers" and forces not under our control but of our own making. Saint Paul called the totality of these powers "the flesh" (*sarx*). "Life according to the flesh" creates a state of existence called *sin*. *Sin* is living our lives merely in terms of our individual subjective aims for ourselves apart from God's initial aim for us, as if we were the center of the universe. As I noted in the previous chapter, a contemporary word describing sin is *egoism*, a condition from which, St. Paul taught, we cannot free ourselves. So *sin* is separation from God and other human beings and from nature, and cannot be overcome by anything human beings do. Consequently, Saint Paul concluded that redemption comes from God's grace given to us in spite of human sin, where *redemption* means release from death as the penalty for sin in the form of a resurrected, embodied life after death. Saint Paul thought that all of this was accomplished through the resurrection of the historical Jesus after his crucifixion, which is part of the meaning of "being in Christ."

The point I am trying to make in this brief summation of St. Paul's anthropology is that one of the enduring theological discussions in Christian history is exactly how the death of Jesus overcomes our separation from God and other human selves that is the result of sin. Mainline Christian tradition, grounded in Saint Paul's theology and running through the theologies of Augustine, Thomas Aquinas, Luther, Calvin, as well as through much contemporary theological reflection, is that God's justice must be first satisfied so that human sin can be forgiven. According to this view, God sent his son, Jesus, into the world as a sacrifice to pay the penalty for sin—death—on behalf of all humankind in order that God can, through grace, bring humankind back into relation with God in that state that the New Testament refers to as the "kingdom of God." This understanding of the meaning of Jesus's death and resurrection is a substitutionary or ransom theory of the atonement. It has in numerous forms been the traditional Christian teaching regarding how the suffering, death, and resurrection of Jesus are redemptive.

My objection to such theories is that they are theologies of divine child abuse, as Christian feminist process theologians have described such atonement theologies. Historically, substitutionary theologies have led to the oppression of women and other disadvantaged minority communities. They also contradict the New Testament's portrayal of God's love as interdependent with justice. My own theological reflection of this matter reflects the work of Peter Abelard's (1079–1142) and the so-called moral theory of atonement, but retranslated into the categories of Whiteheadian process theology. Abelard wrote that God's love, not forensic justice, is the work of atonement. What he meant was that when human beings apprehend the death of Jesus—at the actual time of the crucifixion or now in faith two thousand years later—they encounter the love of God incarnated into the world's rough-and-tumble existence. This occasions repentance because the crucifixion demonstrates both God's love for all creation, including human beings, and the suffering inflicted on God's love by human sin.

Or reread through the lenses of process theology, God has always been in continual interdependent relationship with all things and events at every moment of space-time. In this relationship, God supplies an initial aim that each occasion of experience achieve the maximum self-fulfillment of which it is capable in interdependent relation with the whole of existence. But, as I noted above, every actual occasion possesses its own "subjective aim" for is itself, so that the society of actual occasions of experience that constitute the human self, more often than not, pursues its subjective aim for itself in contradiction with God's initial aim for the self. The source of human freedom and sin originate in the human self's subjective aim.

Again as I noted above, the historical Jesus, according to process theology, is fully human. But unlike other human selves, Jesus conformed his subjective aim to God's initial aim for Jesus, and in so doing, became *the* Christ. One can therefore affirm that "Christ" in the form of God's initial aim is incarnated in all things and events. But the historical Jesus became "*the* Christ" by identifying his subjective aim with God's initial aim. Therefore, following Abelard's lead, reflection on the crucifixion in relation to what I think I have learned from the natural sciences and my dialogue with the world's religions, particularly Buddhism and Islam, has taught me two things.

First, to look at suffering wherever it occurs—in me, in human beings, in other living things, and in God's own experience of creation: here sputters the living, breathing, tortured-to-death historical Jesus. I deeply believe, with Abelard, that this points human beings to the fundamental character of existence: from great suffering for all living beings and God's suffering with us incarnated in Jesus's death on the cross, something other than suffering emerges that is redemptive. The second thing I have learned is that pain and suffering, even as it is redeemed by God, is still pain and suffering, which is always planted in me and every other living being caught in the field of space-time, not because God wills it, but because suffering is ingredient in life itself, which for theological reflection is one of those boundary questions revealed by the hard truth of evolutionary biology.

THE PROBLEM OF SUFFERING

To be alive is to suffer. On this point I think Buddhism's First Noble Truth is in agreement with evolutionary biology and human experience, as well as with Christian process theology. As I have noted, evolution is a process whereby all forms of life—from the first emergence of organic molecules to the forms of life that share this planet today—achieve greater and greater complexity. All forms of life on this planet and elsewhere in the universe, where life probably exists in some form, are constituted by the process of evolution, a process by which random mutations within existing species are passed on reproductively over time, to aid existing species in either adapting to changes in their environments or in evolving into new species capable to adapting to new environments.

Evolutionary processes have led to the emergence of great diversity of species and patterns of natural beauty in the whole of nature's interrelatedness, which is greater than the sum of its parts. But the beauty of natural processes comes at the cost of great suffering. What Darwin called "the economy of nature" and "the struggle for existence," not only creates all species of life, but is also the cause of their eventual extinction. Life must eat life to survive, and it is the fate of most species, perhaps all, to become extinct. But prior to a particular species' extinction, all of its living individuals must suffer and die. More species have become extinct than have emerged from the process of evolution. Furthermore, because of human interaction with the environment, the extinction rate of nonhuman life forms has been greatly amplified. Life is terminal, and pain knows it, and we too shall eventually become food for life forms less evolved than we.

What I have been characterizing is best described as natural suffering. Natural suffering "just is." It is not identical with the suffering human beings impose on themselves and on nonhuman life forms. So the question posed to Christian theological reflection is God's involvement as creator in universal suffering and in what sense this involvement is redemptive. The remainder of this chapter will focus on God's involvement with natural suffering in light of the crucifixion. The question of human-caused suffering, because of humanity's sinfulness, is the topic of the next chapter, where the focus is on liberation theology and social engagement. It must be kept in mind that I do not claim that what follows here and in the next chapter represents Christian opinion in general. Indeed, many Christians, including many in my own Lutheran community, might find my particular theological reflection troublesome. So I do not claim that what follows is normative Christian reflection. But I do claim that it is fully Christian.

John F. Haught's writings are particularly helpful in reflecting on the issue of natural suffering.[7] He calls the reformulation of Christian theological reflection through dialogue with evolutionary biology

7. See Haught, *God after Darwin*.

"evolutionary theology." Inspired by Haught's work, I wish to make the following points relative to God's incarnation of God's self in the historical Jesus as the Christ, as this bears on evolutionary foundation of natural suffering.

First, the doctrine of creation is central to Christian faith and practice. As I have noted, creation is understood in Christian theological tradition as "original creation" (*creatio originalis*), "continuing creation" (*creatio continua*), and "new" or "fulfilled creation" (*creatio nova*). Prior to the cosmological discoveries of contemporary physics and evolutionary biology, theologians did not give much attention to continuing creation and the fulfillment of creation. *Creation* meant that God did something "in the beginning," which, when pushed to extremes leads to deism, or the view that God created the universe and left it to run on its own course according to the natural laws God instituted "in the beginning." But the facts of evolution (and physics) reveal a universe that is constantly new because it is constantly changing, a universe where life is constantly evolving so that every day is the dawn of a new creation. Furthermore, the universe is an imperfect universe, where great suffering is demanded as the price for life itself. No form of creation can occur without suffering. Because of this "fact of life," Christian faith looks toward the future eschatological completion of creation (*creatio nova*).

Second, again I agree with Haught, if there is to be any reasonable hope for humanity's final fulfillment, it must be situated within the wider context of ongoing creation that involves the fulfillment of all things and events caught in the field of space-time since the first moment of the big bang. This was Pierre Teilhard de Chardin's conclusion; he argued that the universe is being drawn by God to a final fulfillment he called "the Omega Point." While Haught does not employ Teilhard's Omega Point in his theological reflection, he more than most contemporary theologians is deeply influenced by Teilhard's views. Haught's main point is that evolution fits quite well into the framework of biblical eschatology. Eschatology will be the topic of the final chapter of this book.

Third, for all Christians, the life, death, and resurrection of the historical Jesus is revelatory. Revelation is not the communication of special propositional information from a divine source of knowledge, but rather the communication of God's own selfhood. As such, "revelation" is a process whereby God's pours God's self fully and without reservation into creation wherever creation occurs. The content of this revelation is God's character as love as manifested in the life, death, and resurrection of the historical Jesus as the Christ. But here's the hiccup: God's character as infinite love cannot be fully apprehended instantaneously by finite creatures in a finite cosmos. Apprehension of God's character as love can only be apprehended in increments. A finite universe can only adapt itself to an infinite source of love by gradual expansion and ongoing self-transcendence, the external manifestations of which might appear to scientists as cosmic and biological evolution.

In other words, living beings inhabit a grace-filled universe. A theology of grace makes the randomness and resulting struggle for existence entailed by natural selection theologically intelligible. God's grace revealed by the self-disclosure of God's character as love in the biography of the historical Jesus affirms that God unconditionally loves the universe and all its life forms, with no strings attached. By definition, love does not absorb, annihilate, or force itself upon the beloved. Instead, love longs for the beloved's independence. The central intuition of the Christ event is that that God loves the universe so completely that God's grace requires letting go of the universe itself. Only a relatively independent universe allowed to be itself could be intimate with God, as modeled in the life and death of the historical Jesus. Theologically understood, evolution is the story of struggle for more and more expansive freedom for all living beings in the presence of God's self-giving grace.

This returns us to the issue of divine power. Of all the styles of contemporary theological reflection, process theology is most attentive to the boundary questions that evolutionary biology poses to theological reflection on God's power. From a process perspective, God is always deeply involved in a universe wherein life, wherever life exists, meanders, experiments, strives, fails, and sometimes succeeds. This implies that divine power means "the capacity to influence" rather than "control," so that "persuasive love," rather than "coercion," is the defining character of God's power. God is not a deity who magically forces things and events to fulfill intentions in miraculous ways that contradict the laws of nature God created. Given God's character as love, rather than being a despot who controls every event, God wills the independence of the universe.

Furthermore, divine power understood as coercive will is incompatible not only with human freedom but also with the prehuman spontaneity that allowed life to evolve into something other than its creator. From a Whiteheadian perspective, evolution occurs because a God of love is the source of both order and novelty. Because God is more interested in novelty than in preserving the status quo, God's will is best understood as the maximization of beauty and intensity of experience for all living entities. This means the epic of evolution is the universe's response to God's own longing that living beings strive toward increasingly richer ways of realizing aesthetic intensity. Or expressed in Whitehead's language, God is more interested in "adventure" than "preservation" of the status quo.

Finally, again drawing on the biography of the historical Jesus, evolutionary biology can support a revised Christian understanding of redemption. The question is, given the perpetual perishing that is structurally part of all cosmic processes—because of the Second Law of Thermodynamics—for what can one reasonably hope? For process theologians, the answer to this question is the same as that given in biblical traditions and other monotheistic traditions; namely, that God "feels" or "prehends" the universe and wherever life occurs in the universe by taking it into God's self. God responds to the universe accordingly, so that everything that occurs in the universe is "saved" by being taken eternally into God's own feelings for the universe.

As a consequence, even though all things and events are the achievements of evolution, all things and events abide permanently within the everlasting compassion of God. In other words, life does not end on a cross. This is so because what the "Christhood" of the historical Jesus of Nazareth signifies is not confined to the historical Jesus; it belongs in a reality known there, but not only there. So while we can truly say, "Jesus is the Christ," we may not say "the Christ is Jesus." Similarly, it is true that "Jesus is Lord"; it is not true that "the Lord is Jesus."[8]

8. See Cragg, *Troubled by Truth*, 208.

6

Social Engagement with Unjust Systemic Boundaries

M Y THESIS IN THIS chapter is that in an interdependent universe, religious faith and practice do not separate us from the world or each other. Instead, faith lived at the boundaries throws us into the world's rough-and-tumble struggle for justice for the human community and the environment. Any theological reflection or religious practice that refuses to wrestle with the systemic boundaries that create injustice in the world, or that refuses to focus on issues of liberation for human beings and for the environment, is as self-serving as it is impotent.

Yet I must confess that like most academics, I have committed my life to ideas that have set me at little risk or put me under few hardships, other than late nights working in my study, or numerous trips to the library. I, and most Anglo-American male university professors I know, differ from most of the world's people. Too many human beings are kept in poverty by "survival-of-the-fittest" forms of free-market capitalism. Too many human beings suffer political and military oppression. Too many human beings experience racial oppression. Too many human beings are forced to expend their energies trying to survive the exploitation of their lives by the powerful, and have neither time nor inclination to revel in the beauty of ideas or in the arts or in theological reflection.

Furthermore, many persons who commit themselves to the liberation of oppressed human beings often do so at incredible risk to themselves. The history of religions is replete with examples of socially engaged persons who speak for their communities against unjust systemic boundaries that cause suffering, poverty, exploitation, and oppression: the nonviolent civil disobedience led by Mahatma Gandhi that convinced the British to leave India; the civil rights movements led by Martin Luther King Jr. (a Baptist Christian); King's contemporary,

Muslim activist Malcolm X; the Buddhist socialist Sulak Sivaraksa (a Thai Buddhist); the socially engaged Buddhist Thich Nhat Hanh; the liberation theologian and Roman Catholic priest from Peru, Gustavo Gutierrez, to name a few. That there have existed such witnesses makes the history of religions not altogether dismal. Yet far too often, the world's religions have been used as a boundary against faithful people engaged in social activism.

Particularly in Christian history, more often than not, theological reflection has become a buffer that justifies exploitation of the poor and the marginalized by the economically and politically powerful. Conventionally religious persons tend to erect doctrinal boundaries between themselves and other religious communities as well as between the rich and poor, the powerful and the impotent. Yet the socially activist traditions of Judaism, Christianity, Islam, Hinduism, Buddhism, and Confucianism reveal that it does not have to be this way. Systemic boundaries can be breached. Injustice can be defeated. But the price is usually very high. In Christian language, to paraphrase Dietrich Bonheoffer, when Christ calls a person, Christ calls that person to his or her death—sometimes to a physical death; most often to the death of one's ego. The defining teachings and practices of all the world's religions have called their followers to a similar death.

For Christian faith, the historical Jesus models the defining character of God as love. Christians are called to unconditionally love all human beings and the creatures of God's continuing creation wisely, as mirrored by God's unconditional love for creation and for all creatures, with no strings attached. Such love is not detached from but passionately involved with the world's suffering, both natural and human caused. We are interdependent, meaning we are all brothers and sisters, since the existence of all life is an expression of God's love, even as life must evolve at the cost of great suffering through processes of natural selection. We should therefore relate to one another according to what persons need, which is often different from what persons want.

But the interdependent flipside of unconditional love is justice, which in the prophetic tradition out of which Jesus lived and taught means liberation from all institutionalized and personal boundaries that cause human oppression and the oppression of nature. Justice means creating an environment that allows persons to achieve what they need for meaningful life in community with one another, with nature, and with God. Or to appropriate Buddhist language, love and justice are "nondual"; both love and justice demand passionate, nonviolent struggle for the dignity of all persons and other sentient beings.

Accordingly, the first commandment—you shall love the Lord your God—is nondual with the second commandment: unbounded love directed by compassionate wisdom takes priority over all ethical injunctions, religious practices, theological formulations, and institutional demands. The second commandment means that loving one's neighbor has priority over proclaiming doctrine, formally worshipping God, or convincing people to join a particular church denomination. The New Testament standard is this: first work things out with your neighbor, brother, sister, or with the stranger, and then go to church or synagogue or mosque or temple (Matthew 5:23–24). Never allow particular religious practices, with their profession of doctrines and ritual observances, to get in the way of doing concrete good for your neighbor, which for Jesus meant all human beings. It's better to break the Sabbath than to fail in loving your neighbor wisely.

Viewed from the loving/compassionate wisdom modeled by Jesus's practice of Judaism, there is something fundamentally wrong with traditional Christian views of other religions, which throughout Christian history have engendered great violence against non-Christians. For starters, the practice of loving/compassionate wisdom means engaging non-Christians in dialogue not as "other," but as persons who in mutual interdependence seek truth. In dialogue, we listen to our non-Christian brothers and sisters with real openness to what they are saying and practicing. Dialogue means treating them as we would want them to treat us. It also means confronting them when we think they are wrong, even as we must be willing to be confronted by them when they think we are wrong. To love our neighbors wisely and compassionately means to be in dialogue with them.

For Christian faith and practice, the questions are these: (1) can we respect our non-Christian brothers and sisters and be open to them if we must believe before we even meet them that our truth is better than theirs, that they are inferior to Christians in what they hold to be true or sacred? And (2) can Christians love non-Christians when they are convinced with a priori certainty that non-Christians will have to accept Christian tradition in order to arrive at the fullness of God's truth? Whenever we hold up a truth claim and insist that according to the will of God it is the absolute norm according to which all other truths must be measured, then we cannot treat non-Christians as brothers and sisters. While absolutizing Christian tradition into a norm for measuring all religious claims *does* enable Christians to confront non-Christians as "other," it *does not* allow us to *encounter* them or *be encountered by them* as brothers and sisters, as loving/compassionate wisdom requires.

LIBERATION THEOLOGY AND RELIGIOUS PLURALISM

Most of my dialogue with liberation theology has been with feminists working to reform the patriarchal power structures of their particular religious traditions. In particular, Buddhist and Christian feminists have clarified for me that religious pluralists and liberation theologians urgently need each other. The history of religions reveals the importance of religious faith as a positive and negative force for social change. Contemporary evidence abounds: the role of Shi'a Islam in the Iranian revolution and its early policy of genocide against the followers of Baha'i, the U.S. Christian Right's support of former president George W. Bush's preemptive "crusade" in Iraq fabricated on the fear of weapons of mass destruction that were never found, the leadership of Christian base communities in implementing the revolution in Nicaragua, Protestant-Catholic violence in Northern Ireland, the revolt of the Tamil-speaking Hindu minority against the majority Buddhist government of Sri Lanka, Hindu-Muslim violence caused by the participation of India in 1948, mutual Israeli-Palestinian terrorism.

Events such as these have convinced me of the broad truth behind the claims of historians like Arnold Toynbee and Wilfred Cantwell Smith: Only a vision that originates from humanity's religious symbols and experience can empower human beings to end the wars human communities wage against themselves and this planet.[1] In spite of the dark side of all religious traditions, it is through hope and self-sacrificing love engendered by religious experience, faith, and theological reflection that the energy, vision, and determination necessary for creating the possibility of a just and peaceful world can be mustard.

This is why Christian liberation theology should understand that all movements of liberation require the participation of all religious

---

1. Toynbee, "What Should Be the Christian Approach," 83–112; Smith, *The Faith of Other Men*, 101.

traditions. "Economic, political, and especially nuclear liberation is too big a job for any one nation, culture, or religion. A cross-cultural interreligious cooperation in liberation praxis and a sharing of liberative theology is called for."[2] Christian liberation theologians have tended to be deeply influenced by the negative caricatures of religious faith in the thought of Karl Barth and Karl Marx. Like Barth and Marx, many Christian liberation theologians too hastily deny the liberating potential of non-Christian traditions. The need for liberation is global and requires a global interreligious dialogue.

An important point clarified by liberation theologians is just how much interreligious dialogue occurs in academic ivory towers overlooking the activities of death squads. Globally, Christians engaged in interreligious dialogue have gradually realized that any notion of practice failing to address the varieties of poverty and oppression that pollute all human communities is irrelevant. Or as David Tracy notes, interreligious dialogue that does not take seriously the challenges of liberation thought in all its varieties too easily becomes a mystical pursuit divorced from "real life in the real world," of interest to only a few ultra-academic dilettantes.[3]

Furthermore, religious pluralists in dialogue with liberation theologies need to recognize the dangers of uncritical, overenthusiastic affirmation of religious pluralism. While pluralism is, I think, a metaphysical fact ingredient in the universe's structure, understanding of this "fact" too easily leads to acceptance of the "intolerable," as Langdon Gilkey phrased it—"virulently nationalistic Shinto, Nazism, aspects of Stalinism and Marxism, Maoism, Khomeini's Islamic fundamentalism"—where "in each of these situations an absolute religion sanctions an oppressive class, race, or national power."[4] The limits of tolerance are set by the victims of society, and the motivation for encountering other religions is not merely the enjoyment of diversity but social engagement with systemic forces of suffering and oppression in order to establish justice for all human beings and for the natural environment in which human beings must live.

For Gustavo Gutiérrez, the term *liberation* has two meanings. First, *liberation* refers to the aspirations of oppressed human beings and social

2. Knitter, "Toward a Liberation Theology of Religions," 179.

3. Tracy, *Dialogue with the Other*, 19–23.

4. Gilkey, "Plurality and Its Theological Implications," 44.

classes. In this sense, *liberation* names a process of struggle that places oppressed human beings in conflict with oppressive national, social, and economic systems so that *liberation practice* means struggling to overcome these systemic forces. Second, *liberation* assumes a particular understanding of history. Christian liberation theologians tend to see history as a process in which human beings gradually assume conscious responsibility for their individual and global future, which means reflecting on past struggles for social and political justice in relation to those that are occurring in the present.

Of course in the context of interreligious dialogue, what liberation practice means will be nuanced differently, as exemplified by Buddhist traditions of social engagement and Christian traditions of social activism. For Christian theological reflection, the central image of liberation is the historical Jesus as the Christ, who brings liberation to all human beings and to nature from bondage to sin and death, but also from the social, economic, and political sins of oppression.

The model for liberation for Theravada Buddhists is the enlightened practice of the historical Gautama the Buddha; and for Mahayana Buddhists, all Buddhas and Bodhisattvas. Awakening engenders compassionate action "skillfully applied" (*upāya*) to help all sentient beings achieve liberation from suffering. Because much of the suffering experienced by human beings and other life forms originates from the structures of economic and political institutions, a necessary part of Buddhist practice is nonviolent struggle against these systems to liberate all beings from systemic suffering of any kind. Awakening without compassionate social engagement is not Awakening. This is the reason that socially engaged Buddhists regard meditation as the foundation of social activism. However, Christian liberation theologians tend to regard disciplines such as centering prayer and contemplative prayer as secondary to the struggle for justice. This is one of the reasons many socially active Christians, particularly Protestants, either have appropriated Buddhist meditation practices into their social activism or have been inspired to reappropriate Christian contemplative practices.

LOVING/COMPASSIONATE WISDOM AND JUSTICE

In agreement with Paul F. Knitter, I am convinced that Buddhist tradition does not have a concept of justice because Buddhism lacks an eschatology.[5] For Buddhists, the universe isn't going anywhere. There is no final future fulfillment; nor need there be. There exists only the here-and-now "empty moment," so that if release from suffering is to be found, it must be discovered in the here-and-now empty moment of the experience of Awakening. Of course, Awakening engenders compassion—that is, the experience of the utter interdependence of all things and events in the ever-changing empty moments of an Awakened One's life. Literally, the sufferings and joys of all sentient beings are part of the experience of an Awakened One. This experience engenders compassionate involvement with the realities of community life to help suffering beings gain release from suffering that ultimately can only happen with the achievement of Awakening. But on this side of the Awakening experience, we can have partial glimpses, and to the degree that we do, we are empowered for compassionate action directed toward specific forms of oppression and violence. This is the meaning of Thich Nhat Hanh's words, "Inner world involves outer work."

Socially engaged Buddhists are uncompromising in the practice of nonviolence, and this has raised for Christians questions about justice. Justice is a central category in Christian theological reflection, while the concept of justice has not played an equivalent role in Buddhism. Christian tradition gives priority to loving engagement with the world as the foundation for establishing justice. So for Christians, the question is, to what extent does nonviolent compassion toward all sentient beings (even toward aggressors doing harm to whole communities of persons) itself become an occasion for injustice?[6] While justice is not identical with revenge, Christian traditions of social justice demand that those who do harm be brought to justice, which means that the establishment of justice may necessitate the use of violence.

Consequently, while the practice of nonviolent compassion as the ethical norm for Buddhists, social engagement has forced Christians to reexamine the relationship between love, justice, and violence; love as involvement with the world in the struggle for justice has energized Buddhists and Christians to examine the relation between the practice

5. Knitter, *Without Buddha*, 180–83.

6. See Cobb, *Beyond Dialogue*, chapters 4–5; Keenan, "Some Questions about the World" and "The Mind of Wisdom and Justice in the Letter of James," as two important examples of contemporary Christian dialogue with Buddhists on the relation between nonviolent compassion and love as the center of Christian traditions of social justice.

of nonviolent compassion and justice. Yet both Christians and Buddhist seem agreed that working together to resolve justice issues is not only possible but also necessary even as the foundations of Buddhist social engagement and Christian social-activist traditions are not identical.

Yet one may well wonder if compassionate nonviolence alone is an appropriate method for preventing *or* ending such horrific events like Holocaust, the bloodshed of American racism, or the United States' preemptive wars in Vietnam and Iraq. I wonder if nonviolent, compassionate social engagement is an adequate response to the three thousand innocent people who died needlessly on September 11, 2001. I wonder if the practice of compassionate nonviolence alone can counter systemic, patriarchal oppression of women, or end human trafficking or drug trafficking. While justice is not identical with revenge, Christian social activism asserts that persons who are unjust, and unjust systems that oppress human beings and the environment, ought not "get away with it."

Christian social activism reflects, not only God's character as loving, modeled by the historical Jesus as the Christ, but also God's character as just. Justice and love are interdependent in Christian tradition, even when coupled with liberation theology's appropriation of Marxist social analysis. Jewish, Christian, and Islamic traditions of justice originate in Hebraic prophetic tradition. For the Hebrew prophets, "justice" (*mišpaṭ*) meant "the right treatment" of human beings, coupled with the prevention of wrong treatment according to the standards set forth in Yahweh's Torah, or "instructions." *Justice* means giving human beings what they need for meaningful existence, which may not necessarily be what they want. But justice should be grounded in "compassion" (*ḥesed*), meaning being so interconnected with human beings as creatures of God that their needs become our needs so that we respond accordingly. The communal expression of justice and compassion is "righteousness" (*ṣedaqah*), meaning "solidarity of community." Justice and compassion reflect God's call that human beings live in just and compassionate solidarity of community, as summarized by Micah eighth hundred years before the birth of the historical Jesus:

> With what shall I come before the LORD,
> or bow myself before God on high?
> Shall I come before him with burnt offerings,
>   and calves a year old?
>   Will the LORD be pleased with thousands of rams,
>   with ten thousands of rivers of oil?

Shall I give my first born for my transgression,
the fruit of my body for the sin of my soul?
He has told you, O mortal, what is good;
and what does the LORD require of you
but to do justice, and to love kindness,
and to walk humbly with your God? (Micah 6:6–8)

Or in more contemporary terms, Christian faith requires that the practice of loving/compassionate wisdom must be guided by the quest for justice for all sentient beings within the environmental structures in which sentient beings must live. From the perspective of evolutionary biology, nonviolence is never fully possible. Life forms must eat other life forms to stay alive, and apparently human beings are at the top of the food chain. The practice of loving/compassionate wisdom seeking justice will not eradicate natural suffering or death. All that can be reasonably hoped for is decreasing the systemic causes of suffering that human beings inflict on the natural order, so that environmental stability can be maintained and in some cases reestablished. But the practice of loving/compassionate wisdom guided by the quest for justice has direct relevance for confronting the suffering caused by unjust political and economic systems that oppress all human beings and environments. This can be illustrated by a consideration of Christian feminist liberation theology, which is also seriously engaged in interreligious dialogue with non-Christian feminist writers.

FEMINIST THEOLOGY AND THE QUEST FOR LIBERATION

At best it will seem problematic, and absurd at worst, for a white male academic to write about feminist theology. There are good reasons for this suspicion. All the world's religions are patriarchal structures that are oppressive to women, and I indeed am a male trained in patriarchy. But nothing remains as it is, and not everything is as it seems. Therefore, it is important at the outset to specify the meaning of *patriarchy* and other related ideas in feminist thought. The two feminist scholars that have helped me most in this regard are Nancy R. Howell, who is a Christian process philosophical theologian, and Rita M. Gross, who is a fellow historian of religions, and a Buddhist feminist.[7] So I shall follow their lead.

---

7. Howell, *A Feminist Cosmology*; and Howell, "Beyond a Feminist Cosmology," 104–16. Also see Gross, *Buddhism after Patriarchy*.

Androcentricism and *patriarchy* usually go together in feminist writing. Androcentricism is a mode of consciousness, a method of gathering information and classifying women's place in a male-defined scheme of reality. Androcentric thought assumes that males represent the defining ideal of humanity, while women are seen as somehow peripheral to this ideal. It pretends that being human has only one center: masculinity. It also occurs in masculine and feminine minds. Patriarchy is the institutionalized expression of androcentricism. Patriarchy always entails a gender hierarchy of men over women. Men control women, or like to think they do.

Androcentricism and patriarchy will be expressed differently in different religious communities, and this fact raises three questions. First, are the world's religions solely a projection of male concerns, experiences, and imagery, coupled with a desire to subjugate women? Second, does *patriarchy* refer only to a system of social organization in which descent and succession are traced through the male line? Third, does *patriarchy* refer to more complex social and historical realities that involve, not only the differentiation of the sexes, but also the symbolization of the natural environment and its relation to the social organization of gender roles with reference to such factors as geography, economics, and psychology? There are many other questions relating to feminist thought, but I shall focus on these specific questions. But, first, here are some preliminary observations.

While it is probably safe to assume that all feminist theology is liberation theology, not all feminist thought is a species of liberation theology. Some feminist writers reject all existing religious traditions as irredeemably patriarchal. But Christian feminist theology is a species of liberation theology, because like other forms of liberation theology, feminist theology arises out of specific experiences of oppression. Furthermore, Christian feminist theology's origins lie in biblical tradition contextualized by women's experiences of oppression. Finally, feminist and liberation theologies that occur in non-Christian traditions are often inspired by, but are nevertheless distinct from, Christian feminist theology. There are Buddhist feminist traditions, Jewish feminist theologies, Islamic feminist theologies, Native American feminist theologies, black feminist theologies, and white feminist theologies, to name only a few.

Methodologically, women who have experienced male oppression write liberation theologies. They typically stress experiential-inductive methods. So Christian feminists focus on concrete situations of women's oppression and try to understand where God is in relation to these situations. But it is the experience of patriarchal sexism—the treatment of women as secondary human beings—that provides the basic object of concern in all feminist thought. According to Gross, this means that feminist theologians who write from a specific religious tradition are faced with "working through a quadruple androcentrisim" in order to find "an accurate and usable past for women" participating in that religious tradition. Otherwise, women have no reason to participate.[8]

This is so because whenever a religious tradition (in Gross's case Buddhism) chooses which literature to keep, and whose experiences to preserve in their historical records, it usually operates with a male-centered or "androcentric consciousness and set of values." Stories about the thought and practices of men are far more likely to be recorded than stories about what women said or did. Furthermore, even if a religious tradition preserves significant records about women, later developments within that tradition tend to ignore these stories and stress stories about male heroes as models of practice and attainment. Add to this the fact that most scholarship on the world's religions is androcentric and often celebrates the male biases of the world's religions and so deepens our ignorance regarding the few existing records about women. All contemporary expressions of the world's religions maintain this unrelenting androcentricism.

The feminist quest for an accurate history originates from the truth that androcentric history cannot by definition be accurate. Androcentric history is filled with omissions about women as historical actors. But a past recounted as normative that ignores or stereotypes the female half of the human species cannot be accurate. Accurate history is better than inaccurate history, not only because accurate history better reflects actual events, but also because inaccurate history is one symptom of oppression. Part of the reason feminists spend time and energy investigating the history of women's roles and images is to recover and recount what is usually not included in these histories.

Related to accurate history is usable history. All historical records are interpretations. No history is an unbiased, neutral recounting of past

8. Gross, *Buddhism after Patriarchy*, 18.

events. The methodological question is *how* historians select "relevant" data. Feminists usually recognize that history is written and rewritten to reinforce values and perspectives a community deems important to its values. So all historians select pasts that are not only accurate but also usable. Feminist historians seek historical models, mostly ignored in andocentric historiography, of events that empower, rather than disempower, women. As Eleanor McLaughlin writes in connection with Christian history, feminist theologians seek a past that is "at once *responsible*—that is, grounded in the historicist rubric of dealing with the past on its own terms—and *usable*. I mean by the search for a usable past . . . an examination of . . . history with a new set of questions that arise out of commitments to wholeness for women and all humanity. Following from new questions, this is a history that redresses omissions and recasts interpretations."[9]

A useable past is important because a religious community constitutes itself by its collective memory of the normative past events it recalls and emulates liturgically and doctrinally. Feminists claim, correctly I believe, that this is as necessary for Buddhists and Hindus, for whom the past is *not* religiously normative, as it is for Jews, Christians, or Muslims, for whom the past *is* revelatory. Accurate history is particularly important when justice issues at stake. When historical records and interpretations ignore women, a community is telling itself something negative about women's potential and place the community. Likewise, if feminists can recover an accurate, usable past for women, the communities in which they participate are reshaped. The stories people tell, the histories they remember are crucial for empowering or disempowering whole segments of a community. Bringing the stories of women into a community's shared collective memory liberates both women and men who are shaped by that community's history of oppression.

When the stories of women are brought into a religious community's shared consciousness, one discovers that the history of women's oppression is very bleak—so bleak that one may well wonder why *anyone* would bother to participate in any religious tradition. Given the actual history of women's oppression, why should any woman knowingly stay and fight the hard battle against patriarchy? For that matter, why should any man participate in a religious tradition that oppresses women? Is it not highly unethical and, if one is Christian, theologically wrong for

9. McLaughlin, "The Christian Past," 94–95.

any human being to stay under these conditions? For if reality, "the way things really are," is a pluralistic, organic system of interrelationships that constantly form and inform the existence of every thing and event in space-time (as Buddhism, the parables of Jesus, the Christian doctrine of creation affirm, and that the natural sciences confirm), then the oppression of women is simultaneously the oppression of men.

Or restated in Whniteheadian language, what happens to one thing or event in the universe happens all things and events; what any thing or event does affects all things and events. Male oppression of women breaks interrelationships that are absolutely necessary for the fulfillment of both women's and men's lives. Just as white racism oppresses people of color *and* white oppressors, as Martin Luther King and Mahatma Gandhi pointed out, so patriarchal oppression of women, who constitute over half the human population on this planet, oppresses men.

So why *should* women stay and fight to reconstruct the religious traditions that oppress them? Indeed, why should men stay? Why not just leave? Some important radical feminist voices have argued that leaving is the only morally and theologically viable option for women. Mary Daly is certain that no woman in her right mind should stay within Christian tradition, since, she argues, the structures of Christian patriarchy are completely beyond redemption. All Christian images of God, all Christian religious practices, all Christian institutions, are *necessarily* male oriented and of necessity oppress women. For women to relate themselves to male-oriented images is antiwoman and antifeminist because there is an "ontological logic"

> which says first and foremost, "Yes" to ourselves as verbs, as participators in the cosmic Verb, as be-ing, which is becoming. This ontological logic means that we are *seeking* our life force, not losing it. We are finding it, reclaiming it. This logic requires the courage to leave the Christian myth and the social structures which are its supporting infrastructures, and the courage to leave is very much a matter of self-interest. To use the image of the mental hospital, radical feminism means exiting from the Christian cuckoo's nest. It means naming the self as good and sane, which will of course elicit labels of "evil" and "insane." Radical feminism therefore means exorcism of these labels (which are applied to all women anyway), refusal to internalize them. It means unlearn-

ing the lesson of self-crucifixion, taking a qualitative leap beyond
the depth-centered processions of patriarchal religion.[10]

The truth of Daly's analysis of the power of patriarchy over women
poses serious challenges to anyone, female of male, choosing to stay in
not only Christian tradition, but also any of the world's religious traditions. Her criticism focuses not only on male domination of women.
Male power over women seems to be mirrored in the structures of all
forms of social, economic, and racial, injustice—not to mention environmental oppression. Even nonradical feminists agree with Daly on
this point; many feminist theologians link patriarchy with militarism
and ecological destruction.[11] Furthermore, there is more truth to this
analysis than most men and women are willing to admit. Why should
anyone who has been on the exploited end of the oppressive power of
patriarchy choose to participate in any patriarchal religious tradition?
For feminists choosing to stay, an accurately usable history becomes vi-
tally important. Feminists have sought reform in all the world's religions
is similar ways, but modified by the distinctive history, practices, and
doctrines of their communities.[12]

For Paula Cooey the trouble with traditional christological images
is that they are exclusively male. Throughout Christian history they have
also generated a rigid spirit-matter, spirit-body, male-female, and spirit-
nature dualisms that have been very hard on the all women as well as
on the poor and the powerless. These dualisms have also been ecologi-
cally disastrous. The body has especially served as a symbolic focus for
much that is oppressive in Christian patriarchy. Identified in traditional
Christian theology with property, finitude, nature, and human female
sexuality, the body provides a major symbolic focus for what Western
culture permits and prohibits. The body determines the dividing line
between public and private. Extended metaphorically, the body creates
social attitudes toward nature. This in turn creates a battleground where
"the human body reflects ongoing struggles for political power through

10. Daly, "The Courage to Leave," 85–86. Also cited in Ingram, *Wrestling with the Ox*, 146. Also see Daly, *Beyond God the Father*; and Daly, *The Church and the Second Sex*.

11. For example, see McFague, *Models of God*, 3–28.

12. See Ingram, *Wrestling with the Ox*, 147–51, for a summary of Lina Gupta's (Hindu), Riffat Hassan's (Muslim), Judith Plaskow's (Jewish) feminist analysis of the patriarchal structures of their respective traditions.

social institutions of slavery, torture, warfare, and marriage. Those who achieve power maintain it by regulation of sexual interaction, reproduction, childbearing, medical practices, and work roles—regulation often justified or rationalized on religious grounds. The powerful, as makers of culture, likewise elicit the tacit support of the relatively powerless through the social consequences of gender, of class, and of the significance of racial and ethnic differences."[13]

Therefore, postpatriarchal images of the incarnation must recognize that the "transfiguration of pain begins with giving voice or bearing witness to injustice with a view to healing and nurture."[14] "Giving voice" and "bearing witness" do not necessarily imply rejecting traditional christological formulations like those of the Nicene Creed or the formulations of Chalcedon. But images of the incarnation will acquire new meanings as Christians reexamine them through the spectacles offered by biblical, particularly New Testament, images of the body and the incarnation in the Synoptic Gospels and in the Pauline Epistles. In these scriptural sources Christians will find images of "ongoing divine creativity characterized as self-emptying imagination, continually making relations, things, and events from the flesh, making these real in the flesh, and repairing broken relations and things by making them differently—creatively, from the inside out rather than from the top down, so to speak."[15]

In other words, the historical Jesus as the Christ brings redemption through directing our attention to the events of his life, death, and resurrection in a way that reconciles and restores all life, including life that is conventionally considered the least noteworthy. Reconciliation and restoration found in the historical Jesus as the Christ have nothing to do with patriarchy.

However, in Mary Daly's opinion, feminism and Christian tradition are radically incompatible. She concludes that all Christian images of God and traditional christological reflection are necessarily male oriented and antiwoman. She also concludes that except in nonliterate primal traditions, this is the case in all of the world's religions. In fact, this incompatibility to which Daly points is not superficial. Nor does it have to do only, or even primarily, with male dominance in church

13. Cooey, "The Redemption of the Body," 106.

14. Ibid., 107.

15. Ibid., 120.

institutions or with the prevalence of sexist language. For her, all these are symptoms of something more fundamental: the maleness of all Christian images of God. Many feminists have extended Daly's radical critique to non-Christian traditions even if they do not follow her critique to her conclusions.

In my judgment, however, Daly is almost correct. Feminist writers throughout the world's religious traditions who have chosen to stay have taught me this lesson: it may be possible for women and men to deconstruct and reconstruct their religious traditions into postpatriarchal forms that liberate both women and men from patriarchal oppression. Daly teaches me that if this is not possible, Christian women and men should leave Christian tradition. For now, the most viable option for women and men is to reconstruct their religious traditions, using not only their particular religious tradition's legacy but also scientific discovery, contemporary postmodern theologies of religious pluralism, and contemporary social and political analyses of the systemic boundaries separating oppressors from oppressed.

My dispute with Daly and other radical feminists is about whether *what has been*, and in many instances still is, remains the only contemporary option. Certainly if Christian tradition is patriarchally irredeemable, Christian faith and practice is not capable of freeing human beings from any kind of oppressive systemic boundary condition. In Daly's view, women should leave Christian tradition behind and create their own religious system of thought and practice exclusive of male participation. Many thoughtful feminists have chosen this option.

But the problem with this option is that it requires "invention" of a new feminist religious tradition. As every historian of religions knows, including feminist historians of religions, no one and no community has ever invented a living religious tradition, other than charlatans out to make money. This is so because as are all religious symbols and myths, religious traditions are "discovered" as communities of human beings interact with nature and the Sacred contextualized by the cultural history within which all human experience must happen.[16] Accordingly, any definition of Christian faith and practice is false that forces Christians to define the meaning of faith and practice solely in terms of past expressions. This is so because religious traditions are not static entities

16. For example, see Gross, *Buddhism after Patriarchy*, 305–17; and Schüssler Fiorenza, "In Search of Women's Heritage," 29–38.

embodying unchanging essences, unless they are "dead religions" like those of ancient Egypt. Religious traditions evolve and become extinct; like any living thing, those that are alive are processes of change and becoming.

Therefore not only Christian women but also Christian men should leave if Christian tradition can be defined only in terms of its past forms. If, for example, Christians are necessarily bound to understandings of the historical Jesus or the Bible that predate the rise of Western critical-historical scholarship, then Christian women and men informed by this scholarship should leave. If Christians are bound to supernatural under-standing of the world and God in reaction to contemporary physics and evolutionary biology, then Christians informed by scientific worldviews should leave. If Christian faith and practice must be identified with what exclusivist and inclusivist theologies of religions have affirmed regarding Christianity as the sole vehicle of humanity's "salvation," then Christians who recognize truths of ultimate importance in non-Christian tradi-tions should leave. If Christian faith and practice must be defined only in terms of its past patriarchal expressions, then Daly is right. Women should leave. So should men.

But leaving is not necessary. To see this, we—men and women— must listen hard to what feminists deconstructing and reconstructing their particular religious traditions are saying and doing. My particular listening has led me to a firm conclusion, which some feminists might find unsatisfactory. Feminist theology is not merely one species consti-tuting the pluralism of liberation theology, although it is that. Feminist theology is the heart of liberation theology because it is its most im-portant expression. After all, women make up over half the human population on this planet. The liberation of women from patriarchal exploitation and oppression is interdependent with humanity's lib-eration from social, political, and economic forms of oppression, since women are generally the most politically, socially, culturally, and eco-nomically exploited human beings in every culture and religious tradi-tion. Women's liberation from systemic patriarchal boundaries is also, I believe, interdependent with the liberation of the natural environment from human oppression. To the degree that women are liberated from oppressive patriarchal boundaries—to that degree—do we all achieve social, political, and economic liberation. To that degree is life itself lib-erated from the threat of human-caused environmental destruction.

A PROPHETIC WARNING FROM JOHN COBB

John B. Cobb Jr., more than most contemporary Christian theologians, stands squarely within the prophetic tradition of the eighth, seventh, and sixth-century biblical prophets.[17] In doing so, he stands in good company—for example, with Martin Luther King Jr. and Archbishop Oscar Romero. What all prophets have in common is standing against their religious community's absolutizing of its past. So it is that for most contemporary Christians, when some idea or proposition is said to be "biblical" (if one is Protestant) or asserted as a declared doctrine by Church councils or papal pronouncements (if one is Roman Catholic), then it has final authority for faith and practice, including for how one must apply these features of the past to the hard issues of contemporary social engagement.

Most of the world's religions revere ancient documents as divinely inspired. There's no error in the Qur'an, Muslims assert, because the words in this sacred text are the exact words God delivered to his final messenger, Mohammed (Peace be upon him). For conservative and fundamentalist Christians, the Bible is the "Word of God," often combined with a biblical literalism that entails asserting that every word in the Bible is true and without error. This contention is often coupled with a second assertion that the evolutionary origin of life and the origin of the universe according to the big bang cosmology are wrong because they contradict the creation stories in Geneses 1 and 2. In the United States, the so-called Christian Right intermixes its theology with free-market capitalism, American exceptionalism, and imperialism.

Secularists are different from Christian conservatives and fundamentalists in their denial of lending *any* authority to the past. For example, as Cobb notes, contemporary physicists no longer cite Aristotle but rely totally on empirical investigation and experimentation. Contemporary philosophers, beginning with Descartes, chose a similar break with the past. Descartes took his own experiences as the starting point of philosophical investigation, which he thought was similar to what all human beings would experience if they thought deeply enough. Descartes wanted to systematically deduce from his experience, particularly from his experience of self-awareness, what must be the case for reality as such. He believed his method would create a reliable philo-

---

17. Cobb, *Spiritual Bankruptcy.*

sophy grounded in certain conclusions. Until the mid-twentieth century, philosophy assumed Descartes's foundationalism while simultaneously excluding forms of understanding reflecting millennia of human experience. Most secularist philosophy today has difficulty with normative issues and *ought* questions. Such questions are typically viewed as subjective matters of preference at best, and epiphenomenal at worst.

In much contemporary theological discourse, particularly in exclusivist and inclusivist theologies, and perhaps in all secularist discourse, conservatives assert alternatives from which one must choose. Both conservatives and secularists cling to their versions of the past. But as Buddhists warn, clinging to anything one thinks is permanent causes suffering. Conservative Christian theologies and secularism have caused enormous suffering to human beings and to the natural environment. It's the clinging that's the problem. But, Cobb argues, there is a third alternative that involves refining and reappropriating the wisdom of the past without clinging to it as we clarify its relevance for the present. He notes that prior to modernity, most critical thought had this character.

For example, Plato and Aristotle began with ideas that had been shaped by Hellenistic cultural experience over centuries of time. They developed their respective philosophies from this history of experience, sifting out what they thought was worthy, clarifying meanings, and thereby organizing ideas in new ways. Most classical Indian and Chinese philosophy followed the same pattern. The past was not discarded, but neither was the past taken as something to which to cling; inherited ideas were critically examined for their value for life in the world. Cobb refers to this process as the secularizing of tradition.

The process of secularizing is at the heart of Hebrew prophetic thought and social engagement. *To prophesy* means to "announce God's words to the community." Most of the prophets were judged to be false because of their commitment to the established religious and political power structures of their day. Their purported words of God were not included in the prophetic traditions of the Hebrew Scriptures. The prophetic oracles that are preserved in the Bible mostly date from the eighth, seventh, and sixth centuries BCE. These oracles are critical of the conventional religious and political establishments of their day because they did not reflect the Torah's demand for justice, compassion, and solidarity of community for all persons. Accordingly, the prophetic voices in Scripture spoke out against the socially and politically powerful who justified their exploitation by means of a conservative religious ideology that contradicted the Torah even as they legalistically clung to the Torah. So like the rich women of Samara, they "grazed off the poor like the cows of Bashan," as they justified themselves through the performance of religious rituals (Amos 4:1–3). Given the prophets' interpretation of the Torah demands, powerful people were the heretics of their day.

It is the same today everywhere in the world in every religious tradition in the world. Economic and political orthodoxies justified by clinging to an idealized religious past not only justify exploitation of the poor, women, persons of color, and non-Christians, but also lead to warfare between religious communities. In every community there is a class of people profoundly dangerous to the rest. (I don't mean criminals. For them, communities have punitive sanctions.) I mean the leaders of society. Invariably, the most dangerous people seek power.

In his novel *The Name of the Rose*, Umberto Eco writes about the odd relationship between the "orthodoxy" of these dangerous people and the "heresy" that the powerful have always known and employed in their quest for power. Reducing poverty, working toward the equality of women with men, mitigating human impact on the environment, establishing civil rights for all persons, and fostering world peace demand the reduction of the privileges of the powerful. So the excluded who become aware of their exclusion are branded heretics, whatever their religious community. And for their part, blinded by their exclusion, the excluded are not interested in any religious tradition. "Scratch a heretic and you will find a leper. Every conservative battle against heresy wants only this: to keep the leper as he is."[18]

This is why I agree with Cobb that the secularizing of the accumulated wisdom of all cultures and of the world's religious traditions is essential to working for the common good. This collective wisdom portrays a unified world of which human beings are a part. Natural processes are real, and parts of these processes are alive. Human life is interdependent with other forms of life, but also distinct and having special significance. Fact and value are not separate, and moral judgments must be rationally justified. There are better and worse ways to live, and part of the meaning of *wisdom* entails the quest to discover these ways.

This view of reality is a much more credible guide than the view of reality one hears preached by secularist preachers of contemporary

18. Eco, *The Name of the Rose*, 239.

science by the likes of Richard Dawkins, or by Christian fundamentalist preachers running amok on national media in the United States and
Europe. Secularists of all stripes react against dogmatized forms of the
major religious traditions, which in varying ways mix the common sense
of tradition with claims of superiority over others, superstition, super-
naturalism, otherworldliness, excessive power in the hands of religious
elites, and legalistically rigid moral codes that often demand irrational
and, at times vicious behavior, as in for example, stoning women to
death for adultery or for disobeying a husband or father in some radical
Islamic movements. There is much in the world's religions against which
thoughtful human beings should rebel.

Cobb notes two forms of this rebellion.[19] One is the secularizing of
tradition. As I've already noted, this occurred in Greece and Israel, but
also in India and China, and has continued to the present. The other
is secularism, which is different from the secularization of tradition.
Secularization entails a rejection of humanity's religious traditions and
seeks forms of thought and practice to counter the influence of religious
faith and practice, usually identified in their most conservative expressions. But the more secularism has succeeded, the more it has failed.
Along with religious fundamentalism, it is one source of the collective
insanity behind the support of free-market capitalism's exploitation of
the poor, humanity's exploitation of nature, and patriarchal oppression
of women, as well warfare between human communities. Our only
choice, a choice for humanity's and the planet's survival, is the secularizing of humanity's religious traditions. Accordingly, Cobb draws three
conclusions in relation to the contemporary crises we all face.[20]

First, if human beings are to free themselves from the insanity
of global free-market capitalism's exploitation of the earth's resources,
Christians (and non-Christians) must be passionate about the earth as a
whole and for the earth's human beings and other life forms. Secularizing
Christian tradition affirms one God creatively and redemptively related
to the whole world and to all human communities regardless of religious
label. It calls those of us who are Christians to express our faith in our
works by devotion to God through co-creatively working with God for
the redemption of the world. Since the historical Jesus modeled love
toward all people, Christians, who have a strong history of dividing the

19. Cobb, *Spiritual Bankruptcy*, 181–82.
20. Ibid.

world into friends and enemies, must reject this part of Christianity's past. As modeled by Jesus, God's care, love, and concern for justice extends to all human beings. If Christians take the historical Jesus seriously, we will not calculate how particular policies will benefit our friends or hinder our enemies. God cares for all, with no strings attached, and so should we, for the sake of the whole of God's creation.

Second, if humanity as a whole is to act in ways that lessen the global social and environmental catastrophes that we now face, leadership cannot continue to be provided by those whose knowledge and understanding have served the established power structures that have led us to these catastrophes. This will require a great reversal that I am not sure can happen even as I hope it does. It will require taking the ideas of indigenous people seriously and evaluating policies by their effects on the least powerful of the human community. This will necessitate basing economic and political policy on awareness of humanity's interdependence and on humanity's interdependence with nature. Motivated by awareness that the suffering of any human being is the suffering of all of us, human needs and the needs of nature must have priority over the economic success of the wealthy elite.

Third, this reversal was central to the message of the historical Jesus. Children and prostitutes, the poor and the oppressed, he taught, will enter the commonwealth of God before religious elites, scholars, politicians, or the wealthy—the "successful people" in the Roman Empire who supported the status quo. The commonwealth of God is based on very different principles. Like the successful of the Roman Empire, those who have been successful in the American Empire think and behave in terms of whatever supports the status quo. If the world is to be rescued from the collective insanity destroying humanity and nature, communal togetherness must be established on entirely different principles.

We must free ourselves from the idea that morality is identical with conformity to a set of rules formulated in the past and religiously sanctioned in the present. Jesus's message is one of freedom from moral legalism, a freedom that intensifies the importance of living in a way that helps realize God's purposes for the world. Love and justice rather than duty or obligation must motivate Christian faith actively working for the common good. This means that whenever rules interfere with responding to humanity's and nature's needs, we must set aside the rules as a means of breaking through oppressive political, economic, patriarchal, racial, and social boundaries.

Breaching these boundaries has never been easy. Perhaps it is impossible. Human beings have known about the need for justice since Paleolithic cave dwellers painted animals on the walls of caves in Lascaux, France. All the world's religions have in their distinctive ways inspired people to work for justice and community so that persons have what they need for meaningful existence. Human beings understand what needs to be done. And yet there has been so little progress, so little that the early twenty-first century does not seem that different from the times in which the Hebrew prophets announced God's disgust with using religious practices as an instrument of oppression—except that current technology makes violence more deadly and threatens human existence and the Earth itself. The collective insanity of the past, in spite of the liberalizing social engagement of Christians, Buddhists, Jews, and Muslims, continues in the present and will continue in the future.

My guess is that the continued insanity of the world explains why the writers of several New Testament books counseled faithful persons to continue to nonviolently work for justice in the human community *and* to wait patiently for God. Translated into a contemporary context, this means nonviolent struggle for justice in the world grounded by socially engaged dialogue with non-Christian social activist movements in the world's religions. For Christians the commonwealth of God is not just past reality manifested in historical Jesus two thousand years ago but also a present, here-and-now reality in the church as it socially engages with the world; *and* a future reality reflective of God's eventual redemption of all things and events caught in the field of space-time. It is this article of faith that prevents me from being a complete pessimist. Socially engaged Christian faith, as my Hebrew Bible teacher, Willis Fisher, liked to say, means "keeping on keeping on," grounded in hope for that final liberation that is the commonwealth of God.

7

The Final Boundary

I HAVE ALWAYS THOUGHT that *eschatology*—reflection on the final destiny of the cosmos—is the most difficult topic for theological reflection because it forces theologians to deal with the fact of death. Death is the ultimate boundary because no one knows *what* death is, but only *that* death is the destiny for all things and events caught in the field of space-time. The problem is that before we can know anything, we must first experience it as we surround it with verbal description. But by the time we experience *our* deaths, it my be too late to know what we've experienced. Furthermore, if it is confirmed that the universe's expansion continues forever, the universe itself seems condemned to pointlessness, and human existence is merely a brief episode in its history.

Still, neither the Bible nor mainline Christian theological reflection stake their claims on scientific descriptions of physical processes, even though contemporary theological reflection needs to be cognizant of what the sciences reveal about these processes. Hope that death "isn't all there is" will have to be grounded in ultimate reality. In Christian language, this reality is named *God*. Hope that the universe and our lives are not pointless will have to rest on God, not on the universe God creates and sustains, but apparently not forever. Because Buddhist nontheism is not concerned with eschatology, dialogue with Buddhism cannot aid Christian theological reflection about the possibility of the universe's final fulfillment. Accordingly, the remainder of this chapter asks the following question: Are there grounds for hope that "this isn't all there is"?

My particular reflection on this question involves three assumptions. First, the eventual futility of the universe over a time scale of trillions of years is not different from the theological problem this poses for the eventual futility of ourselves over a time scale of tens of years.

Scientifically speaking, death seems built into the structure of universe itself because of the Second Law of Thermodynamics, which asserts that in isolated systems far from equilibrium (galaxies, stars, planets, animals, plants, and humans), because of insulation from external influences, things and events tend to become more disorderly. In other words, existence is terminal. Both cosmic death and the death of human and nonhuman life forms pose equivalent questions about the nature of God's intentions for the universe. According to Jewish, Christian, and Islamic teaching, God is the creator of the universe and its laws, including of the Second Law of Thermodynamics. So the central theological issue is the faithfulness of God, meaning the constant and everlasting seriousness with which God regards all creatures that have lived, now live, and will ever live.

Second, evidence that God is faithful will not be found by means of scientific investigation of physical processes, because of the intentional narrowness of both the object of scientific inquiry and the practice of scientific methods. God cannot be brought coherently into scientific investigation as a "God of the gaps" to plug up holes in scientific theories. In the same way, the conclusions of science cannot be coherently employed to plug up the "gaps" in theological reflection. So is there purpose to existence? Is the universe against us, indifferent to us, of perhaps for us, and in what sense? When such metaphysical questions are asked of nature, the answer silence. Yet every once in while, science stumbles upon a clue, like the anthropic principle, that suggests that perhaps the universe had observers like us in mind from the first moment of the big bang.

Perhaps. But it is foolish to employ the anthropic principle as a proof for the existence of God even though some theologians trained in the natural sciences think the anthropic principle makes belief in God's existence a reasonable assumption.[1] When all is said and done, in response to the question, is this all there is? the sciences must remain mute. Stated bluntly, the reasonableness of the hope that God is faithful and that this isn't all there is must rest on wider forms of experience not directly accessible to scientific inquiry, but which nevertheless are as real as the physical processes the sciences describe. So while I shall reflect as a Christian on the faithfulness of God, this does not mean that I think

1. See, Barbour, *When Science Meets Religion*, 29–30, 57–59; and Peacocke, *Theology for a Scientific Age*, 106–12.

Christian faith provides the only valid insights to what is theologically going on in the universe or in human experience.

Third, I do not know how the universe began, and neither do contemporary cosmologists. Any scientific cosmological theory—the most widely accepted at present being standard big bang cosmology—that tries to describe the origin of the universe after Planck time is going to assume that the laws of nature were already in existence. But prior to Planck time, at the instant of the big bang singularity, none of the laws of nature existed that physicists can identify. This does not mean that physicists may not in the future identify physical laws or processes in operation before the big bang, So my question is, from where do the laws of nature originate—the laws that physicists assert break down at the big bang singularity? My answer, which is a theological answer, is, they originate with God. I think the creator allows the history of the universe to unfold from the big bang singularity, which means that the universe does not come from nothing. It is a process that unfolds according to the laws of nature that God creates. But we also live in a universe that will end as surely as we will end. So is it reasonable to hope for a final liberation for all living things in a re-created universe that transcends the boundary of death?

THE NECESSITY FOR SACRIFICE

In *Wrestling with God* I presented John Bowker's description of the plurality of quests for final liberation as a religious exploration of how value can be maintained at the limit of life without seeking illusory compensation.[2] Each of humanity's religious traditions explores the human capacity for self-delusion while recognizing that life yields to life, part to part, and that the attainment of the whole, whether in the forms of life on a coral reef or in human life in a modern city, seems to demand a sacrifice for which few human beings are willing to volunteer. Nevertheless, some human beings do volunteer, thereby making their deaths a sacrifice for the benefit of others.

The theme of sacrifice, which Bowker thinks is the earliest category through which religious traditions explore the fact of death, is fundamentally a theme of life yielding not simply *to* life, but of life yielding *for* life to enable life's possibilities. I think this insight is very

2. Bowker, *The Meanings of Death*, 431.

suggestive for Christian theological reflection about the final boundary that is death. Sacrifice is a major category in all the world's religions, and it is the religious exploration of the plural nature of death that brings human beings to a sensitive awareness of the fact of suffering and evil. But it is clear that differing views of the nature of death and of its relation to the human quest for final liberation beyond death cannot all be true. All may be false, but they cannot all be true, at least as propositions regarding matters of fact. It is not possible for both a Hindu and a Buddhist to be correct in their views regarding human selfhood. It is not possible for both a Muslim and a Christian to be correct regarding what each tradition proposes about the death and resurrection of the historical Jesus.[3]

Such propositional divergence in the soteriologies of the world's religious traditions makes a difference, particularly to those who believe them. They are not trivial, in the way that a preference for ham and eggs rather than oatmeal might be. Thus, Judaism and Islam agree in regarding human beings as teachable: human beings can learn from God through study of the Torah or the Qur'an. God tells Muslims and instructs Jews about what to do and gives human beings help in doing it, thereby educating those who follow these divine orders or instructions into "salvation." But mainline Christian tradition has a relatively pessimistic view of human nature: sin lies at the root of every human enterprise, and we cannot be educated into redemption. Redemption during our lives or after death, if it is to come at all, comes in spite of who we are, through God's grace.[4]

Still, propositional differences between the religious traditions of humanity regarding their portrayals of death and what may survive death may be literally wrong as a matter of factual description. They may also be literally wrong yet may approximate some fundamental demand arising from human experience. In this sense, different religious concep-

---

3. For a brief comparative description of the views of final liberation in Buddhism, Hinduism, Judaism, Islam, and Christianity, see Ingram, *Wrestling with the Ox*, chap. 10.

4. I cannot speak for all Lutherans, but I have very rarely heard the word *salvation* in Lutheran discourse, other than in the conservative theologies of the Missouri and Wisconsin Synods. Lutherans in my Synod, the Evangelical Lutheran Church in America, mostly follow Luther in this regard: our redemption, meaning eternal life in God's commonwealth or kingdom is not something we earn or deserve by anything we do or achieve, or do not do or achieve, but exclusively through justification through God's grace alone.

tualities may reinforce each other, even though in specific details they are incongruent. I do not mean that issues of truth disappear. It is simply that truth issues are not foreclosed in advance. Choices always remain to be made, far short of immediate verification and falsification of factual propositions about death. In the nature of the case, the verification of the possibility of final human fulfillment after death or of the final fulfillment of the universe itself cannot be other than eschatological.

Even so, the world's religious traditions seem to at least agree on one point, in their own distinctive ways. Death kills and grief knows it, and dangerous subversions of the truth include attempts to evade death or to pretend that it is not real or to deny its necessary place in the evolutionary ordering of life, or to structure one's life ethically or religiously in order to reap the reward of life after death. Furthermore, to the question whether death is as great an evil as most of us assume, the religious traditions of humanity *and* the natural sciences unanimously answer no. There exist no other terms on which we can live except those of death. It is in dying that we live.

The religious traditions of humanity, therefore, seem to teach us in their own distinctive ways that sacrifice is the reality under which everything exists—from galaxies to loved ones, who must succumb to entropy and eventually death. Religious traditions instruct us not only to recognize the fact of death but also to affirm death's necessity as a required sacrifice through which life is enabled, ennobled, and secured. Or as the historical Jesus is reported to have said, "No one has greater love than this, to lay down one's life for one's friends" (John 15:13). And out of compassion for all sentient beings the Bodhisattva sacrifices his or her life tor relieve their suffering.

But to what purpose? Are not death and sacrifice, which interlock us not only with each other but also with every thing and event in the universe, as pointless as the blood of bulls and goats against which the Hebrew prophets fumed? "What are your endless sacrifices to me? says the Lord. "I am sick of burnt offerings of rams and the fat of calves. I take no pleasure in the blood of bulls and lambs and goats" (Isaiah 1:2).

Certainly. But not all sacrifices are what they seem. For while we are alive here and now in the flesh, the world's religions teach us that our resistance to the tide of entropy can also create "miracles" of relationship expressive of grace and love, and that in this, we can know that the fact of death is, at least in a preliminary way, creatively transformed. For in the formation and transformation of the interdependent relationships through which we now live, we are already undergoing levels of experience that reach through death, that transcend the experiences of the lilies of the fields in all their glory (cf. Matthew 6:28–30). For some people, this is sufficient, and there is no need to ask further questions. But most human beings seem constituted in such a way that they are capable of entering into multiple relationships of love and hate, or acceptance or rejection, not only with each other, but with nature itself and with a responsive and interactive God that is experienced as both part of us and transcendent to us.

The purpose of sacrifice, then, is to affirm the value of life, which cannot exist on any other terms except death. Affirming that death is a necessity for new and creative transformations of life is the heart of the religious category of sacrifice. This is why we must love the universe and our life in it, while (as the Buddhists say) yet not clinging to it with attachment, because here, as the New Testament affirms, "we have no abiding city" (*Shepherd of Hermas*), because "he is not here. Why seek the living among the dead?" (Luke 24:5).

For Christians, the death and resurrection of the historical Jesus constitute the single event that initiates the life attained through his sacrificial death, a new life we are now partly able to live in the present, but which will be fully lived in the future commonwealth of God. The Christian affirmation of the crucifixion has to do with transformed life beyond entropy and death. There is no final liberation without entropy and death; or in Christian language, God drawing us to God's selfhood has simultaneously drawn God to the necessity of death as the cost God and we must pay for transformed life.

It was probably Pierre Teilhard de Chardin (1881–1955) who was one of the first scientists to realize that the current scientific picture of the universe that began emerging in the early twentieth century indicates that the universe is an unfinished narrative. The cosmos is an uncompleted story. So the universe up to this point in time is in its infancy, or perhaps adolescence. The universe is not a fixed body of things created in a past big bang, but more like an unfolding drama. The universe is not a frozen conglomeration of spatially related objects. It is a "genesis" of continually creating processes that Teilhard suspected was grounded in an unfathomable depth called *God*, which he described as an "Omega Point," drawing together the entire history of the universe, including the history of everything that has existed in the universe, like the concluding act of a drama, to a final conclusion in which everything attains its final completion in interrelation with everything else in God's creative experience. The universe is "persuaded" into this ultimate state, never coerced, as Whitehead phrased it, because God is love, not a dominating engineer. Maybe this is why, to paraphrase St. Paul, death has lost (or is losing) its sting (cf. 1 Corinthians 15:55–56).

FINAL LIBERATION AS RESURRECTION

For me, the question of the beginning and ending of the universe is most meaningfully portrayed in the Gospel of Mark's account of Jesus's argument with the Sadducees, who rejected the resurrection of the dead: "And as for the dead being raised, have you not read in the book of Moses, in the story about the bush, how God said to him, 'I am the God of Abraham, the God of Isaac, and he God of Jacob?' He is God not of the dead, but of the living; you are quite wrong" (Mark 12:26–27) In other words, God did not abandon the Hebrew patriarchs once they served their purpose, but had a final destiny for them. Likewise, Jesus implied, God does not abandon the universe and its life forms once the universe and its life forms have served God's purposes.

But how credible is such hope, given what physics and biology tell us about the universe's physical processes? Although there are strands of Christian theology, deeply influenced by Plato and Aristotle, that posit the survival of an immortal soul that survives the death of the body, I think the tradition that comes closest to what the sciences are revealing about the natural order is the Apostle Paul's vision of the hope for resurrection beyond death in the fifteenth chapter of 1 Corinthians. The issue is not the survival after death of an immortal, unchanging soul self-identical through time. As I have noted, my understanding of human selfhood is very much influenced by St. Paul's anthropology and Buddhism's doctrine of nonself, coupled with Whiteadian process theology's account of selfhood.[5] Neither the human self nor any form of selfhood is permanent. Existence is characterized by impermanence because of the Second Law of Thermodynamics. In this, Buddhist doctrine, biblical tradition, and process theology are in agreement.

---

5. See Ingram, *The Modern Buddhist-Christian Dialogue*, chap. 7.

According to Whitehead, the human self is a series of complex, dynamic, information-bearing patterns that are physically embodied at any instant in the complex societies of actual occasions that constitute the physical body. The self exhibits its own "subjective aim" to achieve the maximum fulfillment or "satisfaction" it can, given the physical and historical environmental contexts in which it finds itself and which it must take into account, either through positive or negative "prehensions." But the self is also "lured" by God's "initial aim" to conform its subjective aim for itself to God's initial aim that all entitles achieve their own fulfillment in interdependence with the totality of other selves. In the complex form of life that characterizes a human being, the self's subjective aim and God's initial aim for the self are usually in conflict, but both operate in the self's becoming. According to John Cobb, what made the historical Jesus so extraordinary was that Jesus's subjective aim and God's initial aim for Jesus were nondual.[6] Or in more traditional Christian language, Jesus subordinated his will to the will of God. In this regard, Muslims are also in agreement: according to the Qur'an, the historical Jesus is a prophet because he "surrendered" (*'islām*) to God's will.

The psychosomatic unity of the self and its physical embodiment is dissolved at death, but I think it is coherent to hope that the present pattern that is me, and the physical patterns of all living things, are remembered (in Whitehead's language, "prehended") and reconstituted by God in a new environment of God's choosing, which is what I understand to be the meaning of St. Paul's teaching about resurrection: "What I am saying, brothers and sisters, is this: flesh and blood cannot inherit the Kingdom of God, nor does the perishable inherit the imperishable. Listen, I will tell you a mystery! We will not all die, but we will be changed, in a moment, in the twinkling of an eye, at the last trumpet. For the trumpet will sound and the dead will be raised imperishable, and we shall be changed" (1 Corinthians 15:50–52)

In other words, life is embodied in physical processes; all life is embodied life. Whatever hope can reasonably exist that death is not the final end, that this isn't all there is, lies in the resurrection of the body. By this I do not mean the resuscitation of our present physical structure, but something captured by physicist-theologian John Polkinghorne's "crude analogy" drawn from computer science: "The software running on our present hardware will be transferred to the hardware of

---

6. Cobb, *Christ in a Pluralistic Age*, 97–110.

the world to come. And where will that eschatological hardware come from? Surely the 'matter' of the world to come must be transformed matter of this world. God will no more abandon the universe than he will abandon us. Hence the importance to theology of the empty tomb, with its message that the Lord's risen and gloried body is the transmutation of his dead body."[7] It is through the resurrection of the historical Jesus, Polkinghorne continues in his interpretation of Romans 8:18–25, that "the destiny of humanity and the destiny of the universe together find their mutual fulfillment in a liberation from decay and futility."[8]

This portrayal of cosmic redemption in which a resurrected humanity will participate is "as immensely thrilling as it is immensely mysterious."[9] Such an imaginable future reflects an almost universal hope that, all the ambiguities and suffering of history notwithstanding, in the end all will be well. Peter Berger argues that such hope is so widely prevalent as to constitute what he called a "signal of transcendence."[10] It is important for Christian theological reflection at the boundaries not to lose its nerve in witnessing to this "signal."

Consequently, in the community of faith known as the church, Christians know the present for what it is—a point of time too charged with eternity to be understood except through mystical and poetic language. By this is I mean language drawn from biblical imagery; from two thousand years of Christian theological reflection; from the experience of worship; from art, music, social engagement, and engagement in interreligious dialogue. It is the only way, it seems to me, that we can reflect while we are alive on that which we have not experienced, even if only partially, if the commonwealth of God is really present now, but not fully. But the need to employ poetic and mystical language in order to speak of what we have not yet experienced fully must not engender the illusory comfort of fables.

For Christian theological reflection at eschatological boundaries, this means betting one's life on—that is, trusting—the historical Jesus as the Christ of faith. Such faith need not imply that only Christians experience resurrection, or that whatever resurrection is, it occurred in

7. Polkinghorne, *The Faith of a Physicist*, 164.

8. Ibid.

9. Ibid.

10. Berger, *A Rumor of Angels*, 72–76.

history for the first time at the resurrection of the historical Jesus. Here is how David Toolan expresses it:

> In hindsight, the church has understood Jesus in cosmic terms. As the New Testament testifies, Jesus has to be taken as a proto-type of or species and, better yet, in cosmic-ecological terms, as the archetype of what the quarks and the molecules, from the beginning, were predestined to become—one resurrected body. Jesus is not simply a moral example. He is, as St. Paul would have it, the axis of cosmic time and the prototype of the fullest em-bodiment of our species' role: the carrier and vessel, the fleshing out of the Creator's great dream for the universe.[11]

The two primary sources for this view of the redemptive role of the historical Jesus as the Christ are St. Paul and the author of the Gospel of John. As the Gospel of John affirms, "In the beginning was the Word . . . and without him not one thing came into being" (John 1:1–3). In other words, the creation of the universe, since creation is ongoing, entails the redemption of the universe. Or to put it another way, creation and re-demption are interdependent. To the original followers of the historical Jesus this must have sounded as if God's Torah had surfaced in the words of a man, because in hearing the historical Jesus, they apprehended the voice of the Creator who continues creating. The Primordial Word (in Whiteheadian language, "the primordial nature of God") was "made flesh, he lived among us, and we saw his glory . . . full of grace and truth" (John 1:14). So the presupposition of all Christian theological reflection is that a minority of one in a backwater place in the Roman Empire two thousand years ago altered the course of the universe's history.

But there is a very difficult problem with what I have thus far written about the historical Jesus as the Christ who brings cosmic re-demption. Holms Rolston III is correct: "nature is cruciform."[12] If God is ultimately the source of all that is and ultimately will be, we directly encounter the reality of evil and suffering. If God *is* love, as 1 John 4:16 declares, and God's love is the power that energized the whole universe, the problem of evil becomes the most difficult question in Christian—and Jewish and Islamic—theological reflection. And while nontheistic religious traditions do not encounter "the problem of evil" in the form of "theodicy" or the "justification of God," the fact of universal suffering

---

11. Toolan, *At Home in the Cosmos*, 208.

12. Rolston, *Science & Religion*, 133–37.

raises profound issues for all religious traditions. Suffering is real—for all sentient beings—and those who suffer know its reality that is often beyond description.

If God's power is best characterized as love—Whitehead would say that God's power as love works as a "divine lure" that "persuades" all things and events to achieve their fullest "satisfaction" as all things and events contribute to the ongoing creative process and to God's own experience—then God is not a cosmic tyrant who predestines events, good or bad, before they happen. Love for God and for us happens in relationships, none of which we experience as permanent, that recognize the independence as well as the interdependence of that which is loved. In other words, from electrons to human beings, God structures freedom into the universe itself.

No doubt, freedom is trivial at the subatomic levels of existence, but for human beings it is not. Human beings are free to reject God's lure to live in mutually interdependent fulfillment with each other and with nature, which means that God will not stop a murderer from shooting, or prevent the Holocaust or genocide in Rwanda. At this juncture, Luther's "theology of the Cross" provides an instructive approach: God interacts with the world, shares the world's suffering with us, and redeems what can be redeemed from the mess human beings make as well as from the natural suffering that the processes of evolution always entail. But God does not control everything, does not predetermine anything, because love means allowing the beloved the freedom not to responds to love that is freely offered.

At this point, the natural sciences can again inform theological reflection. The more physics and biology reveal about the universe, the more it looks like a packaged deal. While human beings contribute to the creative process even as they add to the natural suffering ingredient in existence, we also tend to think that if we were in charge of the universe, we would keep all the good and throw away the bad. But neither the universe nor anything else we know about can be split so dualistically. For example, evolutionary theory shows how genetic mutation has driven the evolutionary history of life on Earth, eventually transforming bacteria into human beings. Genetic mutation is a great good, but this same process allows some cells to become malignant. So the evolution of life cannot happen without the terrible suffering caused by cancer.

Freeman Dyson notes something very similar in the concluding paragraphs of his *Origins of Life*.[13] There is "a sloppiness" to life, he writes, in which life must be able to tolerate error in order to be robust. Novelty happens at the edge of chaos, so that that if something is too stable, too robust, it's just rigid, and nothing new can evolve. But if something is too chaotic, it falls apart. It is on that edge, in that sloppy region where openness is joined to preservation, that life happens. This chaotic region, where all living things must live in order to live at all, is necessarily a dangerous place. But not because God is careless or incompetent. It's is just the cost for the fruitfulness that is life.

I think something like this lies behind St. Paul's portrayal of the historical Jesus as the Christ: "He is the image of the invisible God, the firstborn of all creation, for in him all things in heaven and on earth were created, things visible and invisible . . . he is the beginning, the firstborn from the dead, so that he might come to have first place in everything. For in him all the fullness of God was pleased to dwell, and through him God was pleased to reconcile himself to all things" (Colossians 1:15–20). Or as John Cobb describes the structures of existence that defines Christian experience of faith:

> The structure of experience with Christ, which is bound up with hope in history, is that of dying and rising. Each moment, as soon as it is realized, itself perishes or dies. The new moment truly lives only as it finds some novel possibility, appropriate to its unique situation, and worthy of realization in its own right. Living from our past instead is not a real option. If we seek life while clinging to past realizations, we do not live at all. It is only a question of the pace of death. The one who holds to the past and repeats it does not enliven the past but only joins it in death. However, the one who turns from the past in openness to the new find the past restored and revitalized . . . It is when we think new thoughts that our past thinking remains a vital contributing element, not when we endlessly repeat ourselves or try to defend what we thought in the past.[14]

In other words, it is by dying that we live. The historical Jesus is reported to have once said, "He (and I suppose "she"') who loves his (and her) life shall lose it, and he (and she) who loses his (and her) life

13. Dyson, *Origins of Life*.

14. Cobb, *Christ in a Pluralistic Age*, 243.

will save it" (cf. Mark 8:35). I suspect this is the way life works. But I don't think this is one of God's "commandments," although it is part of the structure of existence that God creates. It's simply an aspect of the human condition wrapped in the field of space-time. So if we "cast our bread upon the waters" (cf. Ecclesiastes 11:1) prepared to give it up for good, it somehow comes back again, but in another form beyond expectation.

God seems to be pretty tricky in the way he deals out grace according to God's creative aims, and there are times when God seems like a card shark dealing from the bottom of the deck in a rigged poker game. But here's the jackpot, according to St. Paul in 1 Corinthians 15: at the moment of death, everyone—all living beings who have lived, are now living, or will live—whether virtuous or not, whether Christian or not, are confronted by the loving gaze of Christ. God deals us a wining hand we neither earn nor deserve.

So whatever redemption is, it encompasses more than humanity. Redemption encompasses the whole natural order, every thing and event in the universe, from the first moment of the Big Bang until the physical processes of this universe finally play out trillions of years into the future. For, as St. Paul put it, "God was in Christ reconciling the world to himself" (2 Corinthians 5:19). The deepest meaning of the universe, the meaning of 13.7 billion years of evolution and beyond, is that all of nature, every thing and event caught in the field of space-time—past, present, and future—is always united with God. Nothing is left out that can be included. Absolutely nothing. But we also had better read the fine print: "I do not give to you as the world gives" (John 14: 27).

Bibliography

Abe, Masao. "God, Emptiness, and Ethics." *Buddhist-Christian Studies* 3 (1983) 53–60.

Abe, Masao, and John B. Cobb, Jr., with Bruce Long. "Buddhist-Christian Dialogue: Past, Present, and Future." *Buddhist-Christian Studies* 1 (1981) 13–29.

Ali, A. Yasuf, translator. *The Holy Qur'an: English Translation of the Meanings and Commentary*. Madinah: King Fahd Complex for the Printing of the Holy Qur'an, n.d.

Anslem, Saint. *Proslogium Monologium: An Appendix, in behalf of the Fool*. Translated by S. N. Deane. New York: Open Court, 1954.

Armstrong, Karen. *The Spiral Staircase*. New York: Knopf, 2004.

Augustine, Saint. *Confessions*. Translated with an introduction and notes by Henry Chadwick. World's Classics. Oxford: Oxford University Press, 1991.

Ayala, Francisco J. "The Evolution of Life." In *Evolutionary and Molecular Biology: Scientific Perspectives on Divine Action*, edited by Robert John Russell et al., 21–57. Vatican City: Vatican Observatory Publications and the Center for Theology and the Natural Sciences, 1998.

Barbour, Ian G. *Religion and Science: Historical and Contemporary Issues*. San Francisco: HarperSanFrancisco, 1997.

———. *When Science Meets Religion*. San Francisco: HarperSanFrancisco, 2000.

Berger, Peter. *The Heretical Imperative: Contemporary Possibilities of Religious Affirmation*. Garden City, NY: Doubleday, 1979.

———. *A Rumor of Angels: Modern Society and the Rediscovery of the Supernatural*. Anchor Books. Garden City, NY: Doubleday, 1970.

Born, Irene, translator. *The Born-Einstein Letters, with Commentaries*. New York: Walker, 1971.

Bornkamm, Günther. *Paul*. Translated by D. M. G. Stalker. New York: Harper & Row, 1971.

Bowker, John. *The Meanings of Death*. Cambridge: Cambridge University Press, 1991.

Bultmann, Rudolf. *Theology of the New Testament*. Vol. 2. Translated by Kendrick Grobel. New York: Scribner, 1955.

Christ, Carol P., and Judith Plaskow, editors. *Womanspirit Rising: A Feminist Reader in Religion*. Harper Forum Books. San Francisco: Harper & Row, 1979.

Christenson, Tom. "The Oddest Word: Paradoxes of Theological Discourse." In *The Boundaries of Knowledge in Science, Buddhism, and Christianity*, edited by Paul D. Numrich, 179–80. Religion, Theology, and Natural Science 15. Göttongen: Vandenhoeck & Ruprecht, 2008.

Cobb, John B., Jr. *Beyond Dialogue: Toward a Mutual Transformation of Christianity and Buddhism*. 1982. Reprint, Eugene, OR: Wipf & Stock, 1998.

———. "Beyond Pluralism." In *Christian Uniqueness Reconsidered: The Myth of a Pluralistic Theology of Religions*, edited by Gavin D'Costa, 81–95. Faith Meets Faith. Maryknoll, NY: Orbis, 1990.

———. "Buddhist Emptiness and the Christian God." *Journal of the American Academy of Religion* 45 (1977) 11–25.

———. "Can a Christian Be a Buddhist, Too?" *Japanese Religions* 10 (December 1978) 1–20.

———. *Christ in a Pluralistic Age*. 1975. Reprint, Eugene, OR: Wipf & Stock, 1999.

———. *A Christian Natural Theology, Based on the Thought of Alfred North Whitehead*. Philadelphia: Westminster, 1965.

———. *God and the World*. 1969. Reprint, Eugene, OR: Wipf & Stock, 2000.

———. *Spiritual Bankruptcy: A Prophetic Call to Action*. Nashville: Abingdon, 2010.

Cobb, John B., Jr., and David Ray Griffin. *Process Theology: An Introductory Exposition*. Philadelphia: Westminster, 1976.

Cooey, Paula. "The Redemption of the Body: Post Patriarchal Reconstruction of Inherited Christian Doctrine." In *After Patriarchy: Feminist Transformations of the World Religions*, edited by Paula M. Cooey et al., 106–30. Faith Meets Faith. Maryknoll, NY: Orbis, 1993.

Cragg, Kenneth. *Troubled by Truth: Biographies in the Presence of Mystery*. Reprint, Eugene, OR: Wipf & Stock, 2009.

Crossan, John Dominic. *The Historical Jesus: The Life of a Mediterranean Jewish Peasant*. San Francisco: Harper, 1991.

Daly, Mary. *Beyond God the Father: Toward a Philosophy of Women's Liberation*. Boston: Beacon, 1973.

———. *The Church and the Second Sex*, with a new, feminist postchristian introd. by the author. New York: Harper & Row, 1975.

———. "The Courage to Leave: A Response to John Cobb's Theology." In *John Cobb's Theology in Process*, edited by David Ray Griffin and Thomas J. J. Altizer, 85–98. Philadelphia: Westminster, 1977.

D'Costa, Gavin, editor. *Christian Uniqueness Reconsidered: The Myth of a Pluralistic Theology of Religions*. Faith Meets Faith. Maryknoll, NY: Orbis, 1990.

Dillard, Annie. *Encounters with Chinese Writers*. Middletown, CT: Wesleyan, 1984.

———. "An Expedition to the Pole." In *Teaching a Stone to Talk: Expeditions and Encounters*, 29–64. New York: Harper & Row, 1982.

Dunne, John S. *The Way of All the Earth: Experiments in Truth and Religion*. Notre Dame: University of Notre Dame Press, 1978.

Dyson, Freeman J. *Origins of Life*. Cambridge: Cambridge University Press, 1995.

Eck, Diana L. *A New Religious America: How a "Christian" Country Has Now Become the Most Religiously Diverse Nation*. San Francisco: HarperSanFrancisco, 2001.

Eco, Umberto. *The Name of the Rose*. Translated by William Weaver. San Diego: Harcourt Brace Jovanovich, 1983.

Einstein, Albert. *Relativity: The Special and General Theory*. Translated by Robert W. Lawson. New York: Crown, 1961.

Elie, Paul. *The Life You Save May Be Your Own: An American Pilgrimage*. New York: Farrar, Straus and Giroux, 2003.

Fiorenza, Francis Schüssler. *Foundational Theology: Jesus and the Church*. New York: Crossroad 1984.

Fleck, Ludwik. *Genesis and Development of a Scientific Fact.* Edited by Thaddeus J. Trenn and Robert K. Merton. Translated by Fred Bradley and Thaddeus J. Trenn. Chicago: University of Chicago Press, 1979.

Gilkey, Langdon. *Maker of Heaven and Earth: A Study of the Christian Doctrine of Creation.* Garden City, NY: Doubleday, 1959.

———. "Plurality and Its Theological Implications." In *The Myth of Christian Uniqueness: Toward a Pluralistic Theology of Religion,* edited by John Hick and Paul F. Knitter, 37–50. Faith Meets Faith. 1987. Reprint, Eugene, OR: Wipf & Stock, 2005.

Gross, Rita M. *Buddhism after Patriarchy: A Feminist History, Analysis and Reconstruction of Buddhism.* Albany: State University of New York Press, 1996.

Halliwell, Jonathan J. "Quantum Cosmology and the Creation of the Universe." In *Cosmology: Historical, Literary, Philosophical, Religious, and Scientific Perspectives,* edited by Norriss S. Hetherington, 477–97. Garland Reference Library of the Humanities 1634. New York: Garland, 1993.

Hanson, K. C., and Douglas E. Oakman. *Palestine in the Time of Jesus.* 2nd ed. Minneapolis: Fortress, 2008.

Hartshorne, Charles. *Divine Relativity: A Social Conception of God.* The Terry Lectures. New Haven: Yale University Press, 1948.

———. *Omnipotence and Other Theological Mistakes.* Albany: State University of New York Press, 1984.

Haught, John F. *Deeper Than Darwin: The Prospect for Religion in the Age of Evolution.* Boulder, CO: Westview, 2003.

———. *God after Darwin: A Theology of Evolution.* 2nd ed. Boulder, CO: Westview, 2008.

———. *Making Sense of Evolution: Darwin, God, and the Drama of Life.* Louisville: Westminster John Knox, 2010.

Hawking, Stephen. *A Brief History of Time.* New York: Bantam, 1988.

———. *A Briefer History of Time.* New York: Bantam, 2005.

Hefner, Philip. "Editorial." *Zygon* 35 (2000) 467–68.

Hick, John. *An Interpretation of Religion: Human Responses to the Transcendent.* New Haven: Yale University Press, 1989.

———. *God Has Many Names.* Philadelphia: Westminster, 1982.

———. "The Non-Absoluteness of Christianity." In *The Myth of Christian Uniqueness: Toward a Pluralistic Theology of Religions,* edited by John Hick and Paul F. Knitter, 16–36. Faith Meets Faith. 1987. Reprint, Eugene, OR: Wipf & Stock, 2005.

Hick, John, and Paul F. Knitter, editors. *The Myth of Christian Uniqueness: Toward a Pluralistic Theology of Reliigons.* Faith Meets Faith. 1987. Reprint, Eugene, OR; Wipf & Stock, 2005.

Howell, Nancy R. *A Feminist Cosmology: Ecology, Solidarity, and Metaphysics.* New York: Humanity, 2000.

———. "Beyond a Feminist Cosmology." In *Constructing a Relational Cosmology,* edited by Paul O. Ingram, 104–16. Princeton Theological Monograph series 62. Eugene, OR: Pickwick, 2006.

Ingram, Paul O. *Buddhist-Christian Dialogue in an Age of Science.* Lanham, MD: Rowman & Littlefield, 2008.

———. "Constrained by Boundaries," in *The Boundaries of Knowledge in Buddhism, Christianity, and Science,* edited by Paul D. Numrich 105–28. Religion, Theologie und Naturwissenschaft 15. Göttongen: Vandenhoeck & Ruprecht, 2008.

————. *The Dharma of Faith: An Introduction to Classical, Pure Land Buddhism.* Washington, DC: University Press of America, 1977.

————. "Interfaith Dialogue as a Source of Buddhist-Christian Creative Transformation." In *Buddhist-Christian Dialogue: Mutual Renewal and Transformation,* edited by Paul O. Ingram and Frederick J. Streng, 77–94. 1986. Reprint, Eugene, OR: Wipf & Stock, 2007.

————. *The Modern Buddhist-Christian Dialogue: Two Universalistic Religions of Transformation.* Studies in Comparative Religion 2. Lewiston, NY: Mellen, 1988.

————. "On the Practice of Faith: A Lutheran's Interior Dialogue with Buddhism." *Buddhist-Christian Studies* 21 (2001) 43–50.

————. *The Process of Buddhist-Christian Dialogue.* Eugene, OR: Cascade Books, 2009.

————. "Shinran Shōnin and Martin Luther: A Soteriololgical Comparison." *Journal of the American Academy of Religion* 39 (1971) 447–80.

————. "'That We May Know Each Other': The Pluralist Hypothesis as a Research Program." *Buddhist-Christian Studies* 24 (2004) 135–57.

————. *Wrestling with God.* Eugene, OR: Cascade Books, 2006.

————. *Wrestling with the Ox: A Theology of Religious Experience.* 1997. Reprint, Eugene, OR: Wipf & Stock, 2006.

Ingram, Paul O., and Frederick J. Streng, editors. *Buddhist-Christian Dialogue: Mutual Renewal and Transformation.* 1986. Reprint, Eugene, OR: Wipf & Stock, 2007.

Isaacson, Walter. *Einstein: His Life and Universe.* New York: Simon & Schuster, 2007.

Ives, Christopher. "Masao Abe and His Dialogical Mission." In *Masao Abe: A Zen Life of Dialogue,* edited by Donald W. Mitchell, 348–53. Boston: Tuttle, 1998.

Jammer, Max. *The Conceptual Development of Quantum Mechanics.* International Series in Pure and Applied Physics. New York: McGraw-Hill, 1966.

————. *Einstein and Religion.* Princeton: Princeton University Press, 1999.

Johnston, William. *Christian Zen: A Way of Meditation.* 2nd ed. San Francisco: Harper & Row, 1979.

Kaufman, Gordon D. "Religious Diversity, Historical Consciousness, and Christian Theology." In *The Myth of Christian Uniqueness: Toward a Pluralistic Theology of Religions,* edited by John Hick and Paul F. Knitter, 3–15. Faith Meets Faith. 1987. Reprint, Eugene, OR: Wipf & Stock, 2005.

Keating, Thomas. *Open Mind, Open Heart: The Contemplative Dimension of the Gospel.* New York: Continuum, 1997.

Keenan, John P. "The Mind of Wisdom and Justice in the Letter of James." In *The Sound of Liberating Truth: Buddhist-Christian Dialogues in Honor of Frederick J. Streng,* edited by Sallie B. King and Paul O. Ingram, 185–99. Richmond, UK: Curzon, 1999.

————. "Some Questions about the World." In *The Sound of Liberating Truth: Buddhist-Christian Dialogues in Honor of Frederick J. Streng,* edited by Sallie B. King and Paul O. Ingram, 181–84. Richmond, UK: Curzon, 1999.

Killen, Patricia O'Connell. *The Art of Theological Reflection.* New York: Crossroad, 1994.

Kindley, David. *Uncertainty: Einstein, Heisenberg, Bohr and the Struggle for the Soul of Science.* New York: Anchor, 2008.

Knitter, Paul F. "Preface." In *The Myth of Christian Uniqueness: Toward a Pluralistic Theology of Religions,* edited by John Hick and Paul F. Knitter, vii–xii. Faith Meets Faith. 1987. Reprint, Eugene, OR: Wipf & Stock, 2005.

————. "Toward a Liberation Theology of Religions." In *The Myth of Christian Uniqueness: Toward a Pluralistic Theology of Religions,* edited by John Hick and

Paul F. Knitter, 178–200. Faith Meets Faith. 1989. Reprint, Eugene, OR: Wipf & Stock, 2005.

———. *Without Buddha I Could Not Be A Christian*. Oxford: One World, 2009.

Kuhn, Thomas S. *The Structure of Scientific Revolutions*. Chicago: University of Chicago Press, 1962.

Küng, Hans. *Christianity and the World Religions: Paths of Dialogue with Islam, Hinduism, and Buddhism*. New York: Doubleday, 1986.

———. *On Being a Christian*. New York: Pocket, 1978.

Lakatos, Imre, and Alan Musgrave, editors. *Criticism and the Growth of Knowledge*. Studies in Logic and the Foundations of Mathematics. Proceedings 4. Cambridge: Cambridge University Press, 1970.

Lonergan, Bernard J. F. *Method in Theology*. New York: Herder & Herder, 1972.

Mankiewicz, Joseph L., director. *All about Eve*. Screenplay by Joseph L. Makiewicz et al. Produced by Darryl F. Zanuck. 1950. 2 DVDs. United States: Twentieth Century Fox Home Entertainment, 1996.

Maraldo, John C. "The Hermeneutics of Practice in Dogen and Francis of Assisi." In *Buddhist-Christian Dialogue: Mutual Renewal and Transformation*, edited by Paul O. Ingram and Frederick J. Streng, 53–74. 1986. Reprint, Eugene, OR: Wipf & Stock, 2007.

Matsunaga, Daigan, and Alicia Matsunage, *Foundation of Japanese Buddhism*. 2 vols. Los Angeles: Buddhist Books, 1974–1976.

McFague, Sallie. *Models of God: Theology for an Ecological, Nuclear Age*. Philadelphia: Fortress, 1987.

McLaughlin, Eleanor. "The Christian Past: Does It Hold a Future for Women?" In *Womanspirit Rising: A Feminist Reader in Religion*, edited by Carol P. Christ and Judith Plaskow, 93–106. Harper Forum Books. San Francisco: Harper & Row, 1979.

Merton, Thomas. *The Asian Journal of Thomas Merton*. Edited by Naomi Burton et al. A New Directions Book. New York: New Directions, 1975.

———. *Entering the Silence: Becoming a Monk & Writer*. Edited by Jonathan Montaldo. The Journals of Thomas Merton 2. San Francisco: Harper San Francisco, 1996.

———. *Mystics & Zen Masters*. A Delta Book. New York: Dell, 1967.

Muck, Terry C., and Rita M. Gross, editors. *Buddhists Talk about Jesus, Christians Talk about the Buddha*. New York: Continuum, 2000.

Murphy, Nancey. "Another Look at Novel Facts." *Studies in History and Philosophy of Science* 20 (1989) 385–88.

———. *Theology in the Age of Scientific Reasoning*. Cornell Studies in the Philosophy of Religion. Ithaca: Cornell University Press, 1990.

Murphy, Nancey, and George F. R. Ellis. *On the Moral Nature of the Universe: Theology, Cosmology, and Ethics*. Theology and the Sciences. Minneapolis: Fortress, 1996.

Nhat Hanh, Thich. *Being Peace*. Edited by Arnold Kotler. Berkeley: Parallax, 1987.

———. *Interbeing: Fourteen Guidelines for Engaged Buddhism*. Berkeley: Parallax, 1993.

Norris, Kathleen. *Amazing Grace: A Vocabulary of Faith*. New York: Riverhead, 1998.

Nygren, Anders. *Agape and Eros*. Translated by Philip S. Watson. Philadelphia: Westminster, 1953.

Panikkar, Raimundo. "The Jordan, the Tiber, and the Ganges: Three Kairological Moments of Christic Self-Consciousness.." In *The Myth of Christian Uniqueness: Toward a Pluralistic Theology of Religions*, 89–116. Faith Meets Faith. 1987. Reprint, Eugene, OR: Wipf & Stock, 2005.

Paris, Abraham. "*Subtle Is the Lord—*": *The Science and the Life of Albert Einstein.* Oxford: Oxford Clarendon, 1982.

Peacocke, Arthur. *Theology for a Scientific Age: Being and Becoming—Natural, Divine, and Human.* Minneapolis: Fortress, 1993.

Peters, Ted. "Resurrection: The Conceptual Challenge." In *Resurrection: Theological and Scientific Assessments,* edited by Ted Peters, Robert John Russell, and Michael Walker, 297–321. Grand Rapids: Eerdmans, 2002.

Petersen, Aage. "The Philosophy of Niels Bohr." *Bulletin of the Atomic Scientists* 19:7 (1963) 8–14.

Polkinghorne, John. *Belief in God in an Age of Science.* Terry Lectures. New Haven: Yale University Press, 1998.

———. *The Faith of a Physicist: Reflections of a Bottom-Up Thinker.* Minneapolis: Fortress, 1996.

———. "The Metaphysics of Divine Action." In *Chaos and Complexity: Scientific Perspectives on Divine Action,* edited by Robert John Russell et al., 147–56 2nd ed. A Series on "Scientific Perspectives on Divine Action." Vatican City: Vatican Observatory, 2000.

Rad, Gerhard von. *Old Testament Theology.* Translated by D. M. G. Stalker. New York: Harper, 1962–1965.

Rahner, Karl. *Theological Investigations.* Vol. 5, *Later Writings.* Baltimore: Helicon, 1966.

Ridderbos, Herman. *Paul: An Outline of His Theology.* Translated by Richard de Witt. Grand Rapids: Eerdmans, 1975.

Rolston, Holmes III. *Science & Religion: A Critical Survey.* Philadelphia: Templeton Foundation Press, 2006.

Rorty, Richard. *Philosophy and the Mirror of Nature.* Princeton: Princeton University Press, 1979.

Ruether, Rosemary Radford. "Feminism and Jewish-Christian Dialogue: Particularism and Universalism in the search for Religious Truth." In *The Myth of Christian Uniqueness: Toward a Pluralistic Theology of Religions,* 137–48. Faith Meets Faith. 1987. Reprint, Eugene, OR: Wipf & Stock, 2005.

Russell, Robert John. "Finite Creation without a Beginning." In *Quantum Cosmology and the Laws of Nature: Scientific Perspectives on Divine Action,* edited by Robert John Russell et al., 291–325. A Series on "Scientific Perspectives on Divine Action" 1. Vatican City: Vatican Observatory, 1996.

———. Russell, Robert John, et al., editors. *Chaos and Complexity: Scientific Perspectives on Divine Action.* 2nd ed. A Series on "Scientific Perspectives on Divine Action." Vatican City: Vatican Observatory, 2000.

Samartha, Stanley J. "The Cross and the Rainbow: Christ in a Multireligious Culture." In *The Myth of Christian Uniqueness: Toward a Pluralistic Theology of Religions,* edited by John Hick and Paul F. Knitter, 69–88. Faith Meets Faith. 1987. Reprint, Eugene, OR: Wipf & Stock, 2005.

Santayana. George. *Interpretations of Poetry and Religion.* Library of Religion and Culture. Harper Torchbooks. New York: Harper, 1957.

Schumann, H. W. *The Historical Buddha: The Times, Life, and Teachings of the Founder of Buddhism.* Translated by M. O'C. Walshe. London: Arkana, 1989.

Schüssler Fiorenza, Elisabeth. "In Search of Women's Heritage." In *Weaving the Visions: New Patterns of Feminist Spirituality,* edited by Judith Plaskow and Carol P. Christ, 29–38. San Francisco: Harper & Row, 1989.

Smith, Barbara Herrrnstein. *Belief and Resistance: Dynamics of Contemporary Intellectual Controversy.* Cambridge: Harvard University Press, 1997.

———. *Contingencies of Value: Alternative Perspectives for Critical Theory.* Cambridge: Harvard University Press, 1988.

———. *Natural Reflections: Human Cognition at the Nexus of Science and Religion.* Terry Lectures Series. New Haven: Yale University Press, 2009.

———. *Scandalous Knowledge: Science, Truth and the Human.* Science and Cultural Theory. Durham: Duke University Press, 2006.

Smith, Wilfred Cantwell. *Belief and History.* Richard lectures for 1974–75, University of Virginia. Charlottesville: University Press of Virginia, 1977.

———. *Faith and Belief.* Princeton: Princeton University Press, 1979.

———. *The Faith of Other Men.* New York: New American Library, 1963.

———. *The Meaning and End of Religion.* Minneapolis: Fortress, 1991.

Stace, W. T. *Mysticism and Philosophy.* Philadelphia: Lippencott, 1960.

Stager, William. "The Mind-Brain Problem." In *Neuroscience and the Person,* edited by Robert John Russell et al., 129–46. A Series on "Perspectives on Divine Action" 4. Vatican City: Vatican Observatory Foundation, 2002.

Stannard, Russell. "Where in the World Is God?" *Research News and Opportunities in Science and Theology* (October 2000) 4.

Streng, Frederick J. *Emptiness: A Study of Religions Meaning.* Nashville: Abingdon, 1967.

———. "Selfhood without Selfishness: Buddhist-Christian Approaches to Authentic Living." In *Buddhist-Christian Dialogue: Mutual Renewal and Transformation,* edited by Paul O. Ingram and Frederick J. Streng, 177–94. 1986. Reprint, Eugene, OR: Wipf & Stock, 2007.

———. *Understanding Religious Life.* Belmont, CA: Wadsworth, 1984.

Suchocki, Marjorie Hewitt. "In Search of Justice: Religious Pluralism from a Feminist Perspective." In *The Myth of Christian Uniqueness: Toward a Pluralistic Theology of Religions,* edited by John Hick and Paul F. Knitter, 149–61. Faith Meets Faith. 1987. Reprint, Eugene, OR: Wipf & Stock, 2005.

Suzuki, Shunryu. *Zen Mind, Beginner's Mind.* New York: Weatherhill, 1979.

Teilhard de Chardin, Pierre. *The Phenomenon of Man.* New York: Harper, 1959.

Thurston, Bonnie. "The Buddhist Offered Me a Raft." In *Buddhists Talk about Jesus, Christians Talk about the Buddha,* edited by Rita M. Gross and Terry C. Muck, 118–30. New York: Continuum, 2000.

Tillich, Paul. *Dynamics of Faith.* World Perspectives 10. New York: Harper, 1957.

———. *Systematic Theology.* Vol. 1, *Reason and Revelation; Being and God.* Chicago: University of Chicago Press, 1951.

Tippler, Frank. "The Omega Point as *Eschaton*: Answers to Pannenberg's Questions for Science." *Zygon* 24 (1989) 217–53.

Toolan, David. *At Home in the Cosmos.* Maryknoll, NY: Orbis, 2001.

Townes, Charles H. "Marriage of Two Minds." *Science and Spirit* (Jan–Feb 2006) 36–43.

Toynbee, Arnold. *An Historian's Approach to Religion.* New York: Oxford University Press, 1956.

———. "What Should Be the Christian Approach to Contemporary Non-Christian Faith?" In *Christianity among the Religions of the World,* 83–112. Hewitt Lectures 1956. New York: Scribner, 1957.

Tracy, David. *Dialogue with the Other: The Inter-religious Dialogue.* Louvain Pastoral Monographs 1. Louvain: Peeters, 1991.

Whitehead, Alfred North. *Adventures of Ideas*. New York: Free Press, 1967.

————. *Modes of Thought*. New York: Macmillan, 1938.

————. *Process and Reality: An Essay in Cosmology*. Corrected ed. Edited by David Ray Griffin and Donald W. Sherburne. Gifford Lectures 1927/28. New York: Free Press, 1985.

————. *Science and the Modern World*. New York: Macmillan, 1926.[

Wright N. T. *The Resurrection of the Son of God*. Christian Origins and the Question of God 3. Minneapolis: Fortress, 2003.

Author Index